D0101605

WAYS INTO PRAYER

CHRISTOPHER HERBERT

CHURCH HOUSE PUBLISHING
Church House, Great Smith Street, London SW1P 3NZ

ISBN 0 7151 0445 4

Published 1987 for the General Synod Board of Education
by Church House Publishing

Printed in Great Britain by Martin's of Berwick

About the Author

Canon Christopher Herbert has been Vicar of St. Thomas-
on-The Bourne, Farnham, Surrey, since 1981. Before that he
was first Diocesan Adviser in Children's Work and then
Director of Religious Education for the Diocese of Hereford.
He is an Honorary Canon of Guildford Cathedral. His previ-
ous publications include *St Paul's, a Place to Dream* (with
John Hencher) for the Friends of St Paul's Cathedral; *The
Edge of Wonder* (CHP); *Be Thou My Vision, a Diary of prayer*
(Collins) and *This Most Amazing Day,* an anthology on the
experience of Easter (CHP).

Contents

The Magnificat:

Before you start

You may find this book more helpful if you *don't* read it straight through at one sitting. It was originally given as a series of addresses in the parish of St Thomas-on-The Bourne, and as such each piece was meant to be heard and read and pondered over by itself. Therefore, in reading the book, it might be wiser simply to read one small section at a time, rather than to go quickly through it from beginning to end.

About this book

I have long been fascinated by the relationship between prayer, poetry and story. Don't misunderstand me. My fascination is, I hope, neither superficial nor trivial. What I am concerned with is that strange centre of our personality which we bring to others in Love and to God in prayer. At that centre words are the only means of exchange, though they are also surrounded by a deep and haunting silence. There, in the centre, lies the origin of poetry, the source of stories and the spring of prayer.

This book attempts to come at prayer from an unusual angle which calls upon the imagination. It uses the approach of story – character, conversations, puns – and by means of those devices it tries to explore, phrase by phrase, the deceptive simplicity of the Lord's Prayer, the Beatitudes and the Magnificat. In case you think that I have no time for the more traditional approach – a thought in which you would be entirely mistaken – there is first a section on 'The Basics of Prayer': God, Adoration, Confession, Thanksgiving, Intercession and Silence. (It's only when the basic discipline has been truly worked at, used and loved that there is a liberty given to come at prayer in new ways.)

My hope is that these pieces may encourage you not only to give time and attention to the more well-tried forms of prayer but also to experiment a little: to trust poetry, stories, and even the occasional joke, as signals of eternity. Of course the paradox of prayer is that although we think we are making the move towards God, in truth it is God who with gracious tenderness comes towards us. 'To seek God means, first of all, to let yourself be found by him'.

Christopher Herbert

about this book

The Basics of Prayer

The best prayer is to rest in the goodness of God,
knowing that that goodness can reach right down to
our lowest depths of need.

(Lady Julian of Norwich)

I have tried in the pieces that follow to be as honest as possible
about prayer. It's a difficult business, for human beings have
a notorious capacity for self-deception. Not only that; relying
entirely on personal experience can be very narrowing. The
fact that I am no mystic, for example, means that I say
nothing about it. Thank goodness there are others who can.
You should look to them for help in that direction. All I offer
are some first and halting steps for the beginner – and if
we're truthful, when it comes to prayer, that's all of us.

The Basics of Prayer: 'God'

I want to begin right at the very beginning, before prayer and
before the business of praying. I want to begin with God, and
to tell you, in so far as it's possible, what I know of him.

I know that God is love. That's a huge claim – but it's the
rock upon which all else is founded. And if you ask me how I
know this, well, words begin to elude me. I sense it. I grasp
it. I know it. I feel it. When the chips are down and nothing
else is left, I sense underneath everything 'love'. It's the way
the grain of the universe goes. It's the music of the spheres.
It's the heart of the mystery we call our living.

1

I know this, not at any totally intellectual level, but by my whole being. Somehow the mystery which is 'I' reaches out to the mystery of the Universe and apprehends it as 'love'. My hunch, for it's more like that than a logical and reasoned assessment of the evidence, is backed up by two things: first, by the life and death and resurrection of Jesus of Nazareth – for in him I seem to see love really at work; secondly, by my own actual experience. As I go with love, as I try to live my life in love for love, no matter how appallingly I fail, then there is a fullness and richness and graciousness and a sense of living life as it is meant to be lived. (I'm not patting myself on the back – just trying to state what I believe to be true.)

For me, then, the foundation upon which all else is built is this: *'God is'* and *'God is love'*.

Now it's the nature of love to want to relate (there's a bit of jargon). But you know what I mean. When two people love each other they want to talk. They want to meet. Let's just remind you perhaps of a time in your life when you sensed the first stirrings of love. I remember I became terribly helpful to my parents and would volunteer to go shopping at any time, only because the girl I hoped to see lived next to the village shop. So I took the initiative and I would do everything I could to meet that girl.

It's not too great a jump, is it, from that very ordinary and delightful human experience to God? If I, as a gauche, clumsy and spotty adolescent boy, wanted to go out of my way – how much more true it is of God. Because God is, and because God is love, he *wants* to come to you. He wants to know you.

What has all this to do with prayer? Well, for me it's one of the basics of prayer. If God wants to come to me, then what I need to do in prayer is make myself available to him. I need to wait. I need to be still. I need just to be there, waiting quietly and in trust for God to arrive.

For me prayer is not a striving after God; not a mad head-long panic through the corridors of eternity looking for him. It's quite the reverse. It's acknowledging, saying 'Yes' to God as love – and then waiting patiently and in love for him to draw near.

That, of course, is what we should be doing all day, every day. In practice what it means is setting aside some time when you consciously and explicitly 'wait'. You wait for the love of God to enfold you. You wait for Almighty God to come close to you – and you wait in love, knowing that God, your Creator and your most blissful companion, wants to find you in his mercy and love.

The basis of prayer is God, not your desires. The movement of prayer is the love of God coming out to seek you – not you going towards him. Prayer is your 'Yes' to the love of God at the heart of the universe, at the heart of your life.

The Basics of Prayer: 'Adoration'

When I say that prayer is saying 'Yes' to God, what do I mean?

I mean first of all a conscious, rational, deliberate acknowledgement of the existence of God. That word 'existence' is a bit dry. I mean more than just 'existence'. I mean the vibrant life of God, the energy of God, the pulsing heart of God. I am not just saying casually 'Yes, I know God exists'. I am saying 'Yes' to the kind of existence God has and is.

Again I take an analogy from a human relationship. When someone they know very, very well has died, the friends left behind don't just shrug their shoulders or cry – they want to meet together to talk about him. When they do so they swap stories, anecdotes, memories. Strangely, there is often a great deal of laughter: 'Gosh, yes, I remember that . . .', 'And do you remember the time when . . .?' It is a great pleasure to savour sweet memories. In effect the friends are saying, 'I am very, very glad that he lived and that I knew him'.

That is how we feel about someone who has died. How very similar this feeling is about our great friends who are still alive. I am very, very glad that they exist, not because of the pleasure they give me, but because the fact that they exist at all is somehow wonderful. A child will clap or dance for joy to see its great friends, and though I am now too grown up to do that, I sometimes could – just because they *are*.

The gladness that I feel is not all-consuming and always existent. That would be unbearable. The gladness I feel is when they phone up or write, or when we meet and go out somewhere together. It is literally momentary – apart from saying something like 'It's great to see you . . .' you don't go on all the time about how pleased you are. That will be conveyed by the way you speak, the way you spend time together. Though it's unspoken, this feeling runs like a golden thread through everything – and, oddly, it's at your friend's death that the thread is deliberately exposed and talked about.

And so it is with our 'adoration' of God. The adoration of God comes out of that lovely awareness that he exists, that he is, and the very fact that he exists at all is wonderful. A friend of

4

mine once said in a Eucharist, 'Let's give three cheers for God'. It was a bit childish, but it captured something of the joy we felt. I probably won't clap or dance in church (inhibited and shy Englishman that I am – though I would like to think it's a case of stiff joints not making a very elegant dance . . .) but I shall sing.

The adoration of God, like the joy of human friendship, is not something we ought to feel all the time. It will be momentary, almost fleeting – but that's enough for now. And our prayer of adoration will probably be short (almost like breathing the word 'Yes' very slowly outwards) and may be, too, in words which others have used: the 'Holy, Holy, Holy' for example, or a snatch of song from the 'Messiah'; or it may be a picture in your mind of something exquisitely beautiful – like a dance, or a piece of porcelain, or the sumptuous curve of a Yorkshire dale . . . and, without working yourself into a false emotional lather, hold that in your mind, and through it express your 'Yes' of love to God.

For in the end that is all that adoration is: a 'Yes' of love – sharing in the joy at the centre of God; entering through the power of the Spirit into the graciously beautiful life of God himself.

The Basics of Prayer: 'Confession'

I approach 'Confession' with some trepidation. The word has such unfortunate associations for some people that they immediately clam up. I am not trying to persuade you to go to 'confession' (though some of you may want to and if so be, then that's fine); nor am I trying to stir up muddy, guilt-ridden depths. *But* confession is a necessary and honest part of prayer. Human beings have a notorious and delightful capacity to delude themselves. In confession you are attempting to bring yourself to God 'as is'. No messing about. No apologies. An appraisal of your faults and wrong-doings – and an acknowledgement that you are not yet the person you have it in you to become.

This is very difficult to explain, because what I have just said makes confession sound a bit brazen. That's not my intention, but I am trying to avoid a crippling, self-centred scrupulosity. So, bearing all that in mind, how to proceed?

It is normally said that if you adore God, you will become aware, in doing so, of your own sins, just as spring sunshine reveals the dust of winter. Frankly I have not always found that to be the case. An illustration from human relationships may explain what I mean.

When I am with someone whom I love very much, I don't spend all my time wallowing in my own failures, inadequacies and wrongs. I enjoy our being together. It's like the pale early morning spring sunshine on a newly mown lawn. It's pure joy.

But when I have hurt them, deliberately or unwittingly, the pain and the sorrow are hard to bear. If you have seen the eyes of a hurt child you will know what I mean. Their look goes to the centre of your soul like a piercing arrow. I have wounded someone I love and in doing so find myself wounded as well, which is, I admit, paradoxical. When that has happened, what can I do? I want to kiss away the hurt. I want to cherish and hug them, to 'pour on oil and wine', to bathe and soothe the pain.

And how do I feel at the time? Angry with myself; guilty; powerless; weak; wretched . . . the whole amalgam. . . And how can I be helped? There is only one who can help, and that's the one I have hurt. The child (if I may continue the analogy) has to forgive me. And you will know how quickly gracious and forgiving children are . . . and that makes you feel even more wretched. . .

This is but the plain working out of the phrase in the Lord's Prayer 'Forgive us our sins as we forgive those who sin against us'. Forgiveness has to be – is – a two-way process. It's about the restoring of relationships, about helping not just me, but the community, to be whole.

In the Anglican Church we make great play of the General Confession, and that is how it should be. Sin, the confession of sin and the speaking of God's absolution, involves all of us, for we are all in the bundle of life together. My sin affects you; yours, me. And God forgives not just *me*, but *us*.

But in the Anglican Church there is also provision for individuals to make their confession. This may surprise you. The line the Anglican Church takes is simple, straightforward, pragmatic and good. It says of individual confession: 'All may; some should; none must'. It couldn't be put more plainly. May I underline, too, what confession is? It's not confession to a priest. It's confession to God, with a priest present to speak, by the grace and help of God, the word of God. And for some this can be a most important and significant part of their Christian life.

Of one thing in this confession business I am certain: we are all sinners. We all break our relationship with God. We are not all as loving as we should be. . . But the joy, the gentle, sweet joy of our faith is this: God forgives. In individual confession, the absolution is spoken . . . and in that word is contained the promise, the bond, the heart of God.

He loves you. He longs to restore the relationship with you . . . do not doubt him. Accept, with all the humility at your disposal, the forgiveness that comes from him. In the sorrow of your confession, and in the joy of forgiveness, heaven and earth meet and you are made one with him, through Jesus, your Saviour and Lord.

The Basics of Prayer: 'Thanksgiving'

The chances against my existing are astronomically high. That chance meeting of those two human beings . . . the relationship from which I was born . . . it's mind-blowing. Add this: not only do I exist but I know that I exist – and I find it astonishing.

That may be a bit heavy. Perhaps I should remind you of Judi Dench in 'A Fine Romance' who locks herself in a cupboard to think, and then ask you to compare that kind of eccentricity with the philosopher Descartes, who locked himself in an oven to try and puzzle through the problem of existence. He came up with a simple phrase: 'Cogito, ergo sum'. 'I think, therefore I am'.

The problem for us in this part of the twentieth century is not the philosophical one 'Do I exist?' but 'Am I glad I exist?'.

Let's begin our journey through this problem at the deepest, blackest end. There are some people who, through weight of sorrow and when no-one supports them, do genuinely doubt their own existence. (Compare that with walking down a street and your friends walking straight past you . . .) Take that experience to its ultimate limits. When relationships break down and everything that I once thought stable slips away like sand – then I face a kind of giddy abyss.

We ought, hard as it is, to face that abyss. It lies under each one of us.

Now let's move to the other extreme – those times when I am aware, and delighted, that I exist: the sun shines; the clear light washes across a calm sea; a child smiling, a joke shared; a kiss . . . on those occasions I am truly glad to be alive.

What have these two extremes to do with prayer? The theme is 'thanksgiving', and I'm trying to see what place thanksgiving has in our life of prayer. On those occasions when I'm glad to be alive, then to thank God is right and good and proper. But what happens in the abyss? Should I be thankful there as well? Often you will find people saying 'Yes, be thankful always and for everything'. I find that attitude unrealistic. Can you, shuffling towards the gas chambers, say 'thank you'? Of course not. Basil Fawlty's attitude seems much more honest than the unrealistic 'always be thankful'. He waves his fist in the air and shouts ironically, 'Thank you . . . thank you very much . . .' It's a futile but understandable and heroic gesture. What he fails to see is that God is also in the heart of the suffering. But that's another story.

Nevertheless, I have to admit that there is something serene and good about acceptance even in the face of awful suffering. I can't solve the dilemma. I merely note it – no, that's not strong enough. I have to live with it. I am not prepared to thank God for suffering . . . but I want, in spite of all the horrors of the world, to thank God that the world exists.

9

Another angle to this business of thanksgiving says – 'Life is a gift'. *You* don't make the trees grow. *You* don't create sunsets. *You* don't (ultimately) make the smiling child. All that comes is 'given', and to be thankful is to acknowledge that I receive far more than I can give.

But the third aspect of thanksgiving is the most important of all.

Earlier I described, very inadequately, the abyss. There is no denying that the world can be a messy, evil and abhorrent place, in which God's absence is more obvious (if I can so put it) than his presence. The only God who makes sense to me is one who, in love, created the world and allowed it to be: who, seeing the mess it is in, offers himself to the world and through the pain of his suffering brings into being a new creation. . . That, for me, is redemption and sacrifice and judgment and love all in one. I believe that in Jesus Christ that is exactly what God did. He took upon himself the sorrow of creation and brought a new possibility to birth.

That God is worthy of all the worship I can offer. *That* God is owed all the love I can offer. *That* God compels me to my knees in adoration.

One of the most ancient descriptive words for the Holy Communion is Eucharist: thanksgiving. *There* is the awareness of the astonishing in life: *there* is a remembrance of the abyss; *there* through the Cross and Resurrection is an awareness of the sacrificial and bounteous love of God. It should be and is at the very centre of the life of any Christian community. Thanksgiving at the centre – and the very same combination of thanksgiving should be at the centre of our individual lives. As God himself is the Eucharist to us, so we are to live with the Eucharist in our hearts, and share his love for the world.

10

The Basics of Prayer: 'Intercession'

One aspect of prayer I would frankly rather not tackle is 'Intercession': praying for other people. I find this aspect of prayer very difficult – not difficult to do, just difficult to explain.

Intercessory prayer is often approached naively, almost thoughtlessly: 'If I pray hard enough, long enough, I can persuade God to do what I want'. An example may help. Someone I know is very ill and so I pray to God for them: 'Dear God, John is very ill; please make him better. . .' I pray that prayer day after day after day, but John does not improve. Sadly, he dies. What am I to think? I can think:

1) God hears me but chooses not to answer my prayer;
2) God does not hear me;
3) There is no God;
4) What kind of God must he be to allow John to suffer like that?
5) Prayer is simply delusion.

Praying in that way bristles with difficulties. I know it, yet I do want to pray for people – I really do, because somehow it seems right and good. So what can I do?

If you read books of collected prayers, or you ever have to choose prayers for worship, it's always worth asking 'What kind of God does this prayer suggest he is?' Unfortunately the picture we often get of God is of some absurdly powerful potentate, who needs to be wheedled and cajoled to do what is right. It's as though he's a king who has to be persuaded out of his castle to meet us poor peasants. If we catch his eye, if we find the right words, he may condescend to do something

11

for us. Such thinking is understandable – but utter non-sense.

Our problem about intercessory prayer comes because we largely picture God 'out there'. We talk about him 'coming to us', as though there were a great distance to be covered. Suppose, though, that we substitute for that picture one which is also entirely biblical: Emman-u-el, 'God is with us'. Then intercessory prayer becomes for me, at any rate, much easier to comprehend.

He is not absent, with me sending up messages all the time trying to persuade him to come home. He is here all the time. Christ beneath us: Christ around us . . . 'nearer than breathing . . . nearer than hands and feet. . .' If God is here all the time, then he is always and everywhere present, and when I pray for others I am simply offering myself to be with the God who is there and with them already. I am expressing solidarity with him and with them. I am saying, 'Lord, you are present with John – I want to be with him and with you as well. . .'

How can I find a picture to express what I mean? Suppose you imagine the love of God as a great and mighty river. Some of that energy can be diverted into channels, if we will but open up the sluice-gates and let it in. By praying, I am opening myself to God; by praying for others I am rejoining the main flow of the river past the entrance, if I can so put it, to my friend – in the belief that the weight and rush and energy of the water may help him to be aware of the love of God. . .

Perhaps that picture's not very useful to you? Let's try another. Picture God as a most beautiful piece of music. The sounds are utterly glorious. That music is being played all the time – but when I join in and sing I add to the music and, I hope, increase by perhaps only a fraction its intensity and richness. My prayer for my friend is, as it were, adding my voice to the song of God, in the hope that its richness may be heard by my friend.

Or a picture from family life: suppose a child comes to his father and says, 'Dad – I know you love my sister and I know that you are worried about her. I just want you to know that I am too, and I'll do anything I can to help'. The father not only feels comforted and supported but his love is also increased.

Perhaps intercessory prayer is like those pictures . . . basically, and at some cost, sharing in the increase of the love of God in the world. If I could move now from the 'giving' end of intercession to the 'receiving' end: there will probably have been moments in your life when you know that friends have been praying for you . . . and you have felt the weight of that prayer supporting you. I know that that's a mixed metaphor – but it's the best way I can find of capturing both the 'depth' of the feeling and the strength of it. What I am trying to say is that intercessory prayer works, not in any magical or naive way, but by 'being with God with the people on my heart' (Michael Ramsey). I am sharing, no matter how inadequately, in God's constant self-giving love to the world. I take part in that great procession of love.

For me then, intercession is as simple and as difficult as that . . . and its results are immeasurable, unknown, hidden deep in the heart and mind of God. All that any of us can do (but it's desperately hard and a *daily* task) is to pray as Jesus did: 'Father . . . thy will be done'. If all of us could intercede like that – offering our very selves to God for our fellow men – then, in the life of the Holy Spirit, we should be sharing in the self-giving and redeeming love of Jesus the Saviour.

The Basics of Prayer: 'Silence'

I have written about God and adoration and confession and thanksgiving and supplication. So what is there left? The impossible task, a task verging on absurdity: I want to discuss silence.

I was made very aware of the difficulty and absurdity of this once at a prayer meeting, where someone said, 'Lord, thank you for silence, for the times of stillness and beauty; thank you that in silence we can hear you . . . the silence is wonderful'. He went on and on about silence, leaving no space at all for any of us to be silent in. (No doubt God enjoyed the joke too.)

So: into silence. There are some buildings you enter which have a quality of silence that almost knocks you over. I think of some of our great cathedrals – say, Wells late on a summer evening – or of the Chapel at Taizé. You go into those buildings all of a rush and a clatter, and are brought to a full stop. Your pace is slowed down. You have to pause and look around you: a kind of sudden, unexpected spiritual holiday. I would venture to suggest that the stillness is not simply architectural. It is because those places are holy, places of prayer. The very stones are steeped in prayer ('You are here to kneel where prayer has been valid'.)

If buildings can have that quality, so can certain people: people of great spiritual depth and loveliness who are simply good to be with. How can you attain that kind of spiritual stillness? Well, let's point out the obvious. It isn't achieved overnight – it takes years and years and years of patient and faithful waiting upon God; and if, in his grace, you have that inner stillness, you may not even be aware of it – God is very wise.

14

So to be practical. How do you start to learn stillness? First of all, you have a body and for good and ill you have to come to terms with it. In prayer, your body will be a constant reminder to you of your limitations. So if you want to be really still and silent, you need to get your body organised. How you do this will be your affair. Basically, what you are after is to get yourself comfortable without being slumped, and attentive without being highly anxious. Personally I find that sitting upright, 'hands together, and eyes closed', is the best for me.

Then what? Well, give your body time to settle down. You've chased it around all day – don't expect it suddenly to stop and be calm at the press of a button. Be gentle with yourself . . . and give your body time just to calm down and be still. Don't expect, either, that you can achieve this instantly. Learning this kind of stillness is a long process, and one which requires repetition, grace and faithfulness. If nothing happens in your mind, so be it; your wanting to be still and be at prayer is prayer in itself.

You need to allow yourself a time and a place. Begin with five minutes' silence every day – and gradually extend this period if you can, until you can spend half-an-hour. If you find that you want to spend even longer in silence, then that will be the time to find yourself a Spiritual Director – someone who will guide and help you in the way your prayer should go.

As far as finding a place for silence, that's not always so easy. Only you can know where is best for you. Don't overlook your local church. It needs to be prayed in. Once you have found a place, once you have made a regular time for silence, then what? You could begin by thinking of a brief phrase: 'Be still and know that I am God' or 'Lord, have mercy' – and pray that phrase in time with your breathing. (Again, you would be wise to seek spiritual advice as this develops.) And then just wait – wait attentively and with love upon God.

If your thoughts wander – so be it. Don't get angry with yourself and try to rein yourself back into the road. That's just punishing yourself. You will find that your soul, the real depths of you, will gradually learn to be attentive at a level deeper than those day-dreams (in any case much of our day-dreaming is necessary. . .).

Just wait, quietly, silently upon God. He looks upon you with tenderness and love. You don't need to talk your way into his presence like a garrulous sales rep, nor do you have to wheedle and cajole, nor do you have to apologise for your own existence.

In the silence, what you are doing is acknowledging with love the presence of God who, in his turn, loves you with the sweetest, most courteous, most disarming love. In silence you are you and you look at God – and God looks at you and comes to you with his wounded hands outstretched to embrace you. And the paradox is that in that embrace you do not cease to have any identity; your identity, if I can so put it, is strengthened and cherished and encouraged. Love gives you new life at the depth of your being – the life which lasts to eternity.

The Lord's Prayer

Once, in a certain place, Jesus was at prayer. When he
ceased, one of his disciples said, 'Lord, teach us to
pray, as John taught his disciples.' He answered,
'When you pray, say . . .'

(Luke 11.1)

The Lord's Prayer is so familiar that to approach it through
traditional ways would not be helpful, and so I have constructed what is more like a meditation than a commentary.
Shaped as a conversation (in the first part the speaker is
Everyman; in the second part the reply comes from God), the
meditation nevertheless is based as carefully as possible on
contemporary scholarship and research. The format of the
conversation between Everyman and God is not new; Lady
Julian of Norwich used it centuries ago, and in our own time
Michel Quoist has re-popularised it.

Our Father . . .

In this first 'meditation' you have to imagine the opening
scene. Everyman, who may be Everywoman, comes into
church and kneels to pray. What follows are those random
thoughts, which we all have, that muddle themselves into our
attempts to pray:

Everyman speaks:

Right, Lord: so here we are. I've successfully negotiated the
conversations in the porch, picked up a broadsheet – (if

17

there are any more puns from the Vicar I shall scream, so help me) and I have chosen, thank heaven, my favourite seat. Now, where was I? Right – Lord, I'm about to pray – what shall I say? You can't be interested in that gossip I heard in Sainsbury's, but I agree, if she'd had any sense, she'd have known better. . . My knee, Lord. It's getting worse. I'm sure it's stiffer today than it's been for weeks. Maybe a thermal bandage, or one of those copper bracelets. . .

Oh, goodness, someone wants to come past. I'm praying, can't they see? Can't they go round the other side? In any case there's something very embarrassing about being close to a complete stranger: you know what I mean – especially if their shoes squeak. I want to giggle. Anyway I shall get up, smile, let them in and then perhaps kneel down again. . .

On the other hand sitting, you have to admit, is so much more comfortable, especially on chairs. Pews – give me pews for kneeling, any day. You can really rest yourself on pews. But chairs – you're always worried in case you move them or, heaven forbid, knock your forehead against the back of the person in front. That, if I may say so, is more embarrassing than anything else; you can feel them tense. Far too close. I shall suggest it to the Vicar: chairs out, pews in. Lord, where was I?

Ah, yes: praying. Right, Lord – here we go. 'God' – no, 'Almighty God'. Better – more reverent. Like talking to the Queen. Isn't she lovely? And her mother? All those powder-blues and yellows. God bless the Queen Mum. But why she has those yapping corgis I don't know. A labrador, yes, but not those corgis. Sorry, Lord: only there was this lovely picture in the *Mail*. She was wearing a headscarf. They were off on holiday and there were leads everywhere. They deserve a break. Good luck to them. . .

18

Lord, here I go again, rabbiting on – and I only came here to get a bit of peace and quiet and my mind won't stay still. My indigestion has calmed down a bit (shall I unwrap the Rennie now or during the sermon?) – but, Lord, if only I could calm down, quieten myself, not rush, rush, rush. . .

I shall try again. 'Almighty God' . . . if only the door would stop opening and closing, I could pray. I really could. But then, come to think of it, I've never been taught. To pray, I mean. No one has ever said to me: 'This is how you should pray'. I need a course on 'how to pray' techniques/deep breathing/concentration.

If only I knew the right techniques. I'm sure there must be a book somewhere. And if only . . . if only I could concentrate. Oh, dear Lord: teach me to pray.

God replies:

Do you suppose, my loving child, that I'm interested in techniques? Techniques can get in the way. You can spend so much time and energy wondering whether your posture's right, or whether you're breathing correctly that you forget what prayer is for. I am not interested in whether or not you master techniques. Prayer is greater than that.

Do not worry about the concentration. Why do you suppose I made you as a dreamer? Human beings have some strange ideas. They seem to think that dreaming is a subtle subterfuge – designed (they never ask 'by whom?') to lead them astray. Then they try to concentrate like mad. Furrowed brows. Concentrate. Concentrate. I love them for their 'work': but I'm not found that way . . . at least, not by many. Honestly, praying is not a fitness exercise: a way of developing spiritual muscles.

19

As for your knees and indigestion: 'tempus fugit'. I know it's painful and a nuisance and if the pain keeps breaking through, accept it. That too can be a form of prayer.

The thing is this: I want you to pray. I'll repeat that: I want you to pray. Not techniques, not beautifully constructed cadences – you can enjoy those later; I just want you to pray. And prayer is very simple: talk to me. That's all. Just talk to me; like you would to a Father or a Mother. For that is who I am; what I am. I shall listen to you. Really listen. I shall hear the words, the spaces between the words, and those sorrows and joys that are beyond words. The sighs from your soul. I hear those. . .

You are, you lovely, muddle-headed, topsy-turvy, gorgeous, clowning, sorrowful person (you see even I don't use sexist language any more!) – you are my child. I brought you into being. In love I hold you in being – and gradually, ever so gradually, like a rose unfolding I shall disclose my very self to you. Don't be impatient to know me. I shall enable you to see who I am in ways which are right for you and in good time. . .

And yes, I do know what you are really like. I do know your darkness: I know your anger, your bitterness: I know your malevolence. I know all that. The darkness is as much you as the light – but the darkness of the soil is as necessary for growth as the sunshine, isn't it?

Through Jesus Christ I have shown you who I am. So when you come to me, use his words, and say: 'Father . . .' For that is the truth.

Hallowed be thy name . . .

It's the end of the day. You're sitting in an armchair simply reflecting upon all the things that have happened . . . and you dream a few dreams, or say a few prayers (whichever you consider these reflections to be . . .). In the background there's the gentle tick-tock of a grandfather clock and at your feet a cat – half asleep and twitching its ears occasionally. . .

Everyman speaks:

Lord, what a day . . . I think I shall give up watching the news. I can't stand it much more: those poor, poor children, dry-eyed and pot-bellied; and their mothers! They could be me . . . I could be them . . . resigned with unutterable weariness to the pain of the world. I cry for them. Not real tears I admit – but with a sigh from my soul. . .

And then Northern Ireland. So help me, I don't even flinch at the deaths any more. I have become used to the violence, the stupidity, the barbarity . . . once I was angry, but the wells of anger have dried up. I can't help it. I yearn for their peace, for a solution, for a spark of hope. . .

As for the strikers and the managements and the truths and half-truths, I don't know what to think. The hard facts of economics are just that – hard; but I see and value the importance of community, of sticking together against 'them'. And I know it's sometimes narrow-minded bigotry: but it can also be warmth and care and roots. . .

(The cat stirs – stretches, yawns, turns to the fire and rests its head on its front paw.)

Lord, I envy that cat. No cares. No worries. No imagination. Fed, watered, loved. If I could be as relaxed as that . . . look at him. At peace. At home.

Which reminds me . . .

My grandson. I don't know what will become of him. Honestly I don't. Young people these days baffle me. He's so kind sometimes, far kinder than I ever was at his age, and at other times he's ruthless. Totally selfish, his mother says. Shouting and stamping and getting drunk. At least he's not on drugs . . . but, Lord, I fear for him. I fear for the world he's growing up in. Has he anything to hope for?

If only they lived a bit nearer. Because, Lord, I know this is a moan and I know it's ever so selfish, but sometimes the loneliness is unbearable. It's like a lead weight inside you. No: not quite. An emptiness that is heavy. Can you understand? An emptiness that threatens to crush me. I ache. An ache so deep. A wound. I am wounded, Lord, at the centre of my being. Pierced. Afraid. And sometimes so unhappy . . . well. If that's selfish, Lord, so be it. But honestly, sometimes, *only* sometimes, it's all too much.

Perhaps it comes from a too close acquaintanceship with death. I go to more funerals now than parties and sit with my friends wondering whose turn's next.

(The cat moves, extending its forepaws to scrabble at the carpet. Hauls itself along on its side in sheer ecstasy. Gets up – licks itself. Looks as though it's about to make a great decision. Pauses. Lies back down again and goes to sleep. . .)

Time for bed, Lord . . . 'Hallowed be thy Name.'

God replies:

My lovely child, I know. I know. I am with you at the heart of it all. I am the sigh from your soul. I am the ache at the centre of your being. I am the piercing and the sorrow; I am the emptiness. I am the wound.

22

Do the children starve and I am not moved? When the bombs blast am I not injured? Are the insults hurled and I am not pained? Are you afraid and I do not understand? Are you broken in heart and I am not hurt?

For is not all this the cost of love, the cost of knowing? But in there, in the ache and the piercing, in the sorrow and the wound – in there, I am.

– and that is the hallowing.

Not a divine ego-trip for me. I don't want flattery. My name is not hallowed by the clichéd phrase. I am not touched by empty praises. Do you think I created you to fawn upon me? I am not hallowed by that. . .

The way of hallowing is the way of deepening, for in the depths you will discover me: in the depths of love, in the depths of sorrow, in the depths of truth, in the depths of beauty . . . there in the depths I am, and beyond the depth itself . . . I shall call you.

My name is hallowed as you draw close to me . . . as you in your life share in the wounds of Christ and in his compassion.

My name is hallowed as you, through your wandering, become a healer for the wounds of others. . .

You will hallow my name as you become love; you will hallow my name as you share in the redemption of the world.

Father, hallowed be thy Name. . .

Thy kingdom come . . .

Everyman speaks:

I love trains. No, that's not exactly true. What I love are train journeys. They have everything you want: company (have you noticed the infinite variety of the human face: long noses, short noses, sad eyes, joyful eyes?), talk (lots and lots of gossipy talk), and a constantly changing view. God bless the makers of trains.

And what is more, trains are good places for praying. I don't mean eyes closed, hands together, concentrated prayer; I mean long, languorous dreamy prayers. Oh yes, a few arrow-prayers shot up into the wide blue yonder from time to time – but mostly 'looking prayers'. You know, simply getting pleasure from the fact that something *is:* that the bricks on Aldershot station are creamy-grey; that the wrought iron supporting the roof is heavy and workmanlike but has a sense of humour. (We don't have jokes in buildings any more: take ourselves far too seriously.) That's what a looking-prayer is: a recognition of the there-ness of things.

Well, isn't that so, Lord? I mean isn't it the case that if I look at something with honesty and appreciation, it's a way of loving? Look: this could be sentimental, I know. It could be all sunsets and clouds and Jonathan Livingston Seagull. Which reminds me of one of those posters –there were two seagulls gliding, and the legend said, 'They can because they think they can.' And someone had scribbled underneath, 'And because they've got wings.'

Where was I, Lord? Ah, yes. 'Looking prayers.' If I could see the world through your eyes . . . that's what I want to do. See it as you see it. See colours as vividly as you do. See glory in a

24

dandelion. Sort of clapping silently and secretly because something *is*.

Look, Lord, I'll get to the point: I think that you are everywhere. Do you know what I mean? I think you are in sunshine and laughter, in the sweet grace of a birch tree, in fields and meadows, in the song of a blackbird on the edge of a wood (see – I read my T. S. Eliot). You, God, are everywhere, aren't you? So when I pray 'Thy kingdom come', I'm saying my 'Yes' to the you-ness of you.

I shall shut up now, Lord. It's time I did. Too many words. Not enough space between the bars. . .

God replies:

My loving child, what a funny, muddle-headed dreamer you are. . .

Of course I'm in the fields and, as you put it, in the glory of the dandelion. (Mind you, I reckon that was going over the top a bit.) Of course, I'm in the birch tree and the blackbird on the edge of the wood. I am there in the 'thereness' of things.

And yes: you do need to open your eyes. But do not ask to see the world through my eyes. Could you bear the sorrow? Could you carry the anguish? To see the world with my eyes is to see it through the mist of tears. And that's not for you to do: I know your limits: allow me to be me. Allow me to carry all that: and allow yourself to see the world with the eyes I have given you. The amount you can see is right for you – and what you can see in the fields and the hedgerows is a part of my kingdom. . .

But, if I may say so, I think your view of the kingdom is a little one-sided. Beautifully English: straight from Wordsworth. . . My kingdom, however, is also about justice and mercy and truth. My kingdom is Ethiopia as well as the Lake District. My kingdom is under the arches of Hungerford Bridge; in the sightless of Bhopal; in the barbarity of torture and imprisonment; my kingdom is found wherever the hungry are fed; wherever suffering is relieved; wherever prisoners are released; wherever relationships are healed; wherever the blind receive their sight.

When you pray for my kingdom you are standing alongside me: committing yourself to the relief of need, to the broken in spirit and the humble in heart. When you pray for my kingdom you will feel the weight of the cross settle on your shoulders. When you pray for my kingdom you will see the Easter light break over the horizon and a dove flying towards you. . .

Thy will be done on earth as it is in heaven . . .

The scene is a family sitting-room an hour or so before a funeral. The widower, an old man, is sitting on an upright chair next to a table. He is dressed already, shaved (he cut himself, but the blood has dried), and wearing a suit which he refers to as his 'funeral suit'. He looks ill at ease in it. Lost inside it. His new white shirt has a collar that's too stiff. It digs into his neck and from time to time he runs a finger under it to loosen it. His shoes are polished brilliantly. His only daughter, a woman in her late fifties, is busy in the kitchen, cutting sandwiches, checking the plates. He looks

26

out of the window on to a small lawn. A few sparrows are quarrelling over some bread. He prays:

'Lord, I don't know what to say. Got nothing to say. Feel empty, numb and frightened to death (forgive the phrase). She was lovely, a real lady. And kind. Kind. She'd have given the house away and me with it. I remember her saying that once: 'Got a jumble sale,' she said. 'I'm thinking of taking you.' He winced at the memory and smiled at the same time.

'All right, Dad?' The daughter bustled in with some cups and saucers. She didn't know whether to try to comfort him or not, and decided against it.

'Yes, thank you.' He continued to look out of the window. 'The birds'll miss her. Bread every morning, and scraps of bacon.' He could see her now, the way she held the bread-knife in her right hand, loaf in her left and cut towards her. It always looked dangerous. He had given up commenting on it years ago. 'Have I ever cut myself?' she'd say. 'And look at your face. It's like a battlefield. You've no right to talk.' And he'd done the same this morning. She would have smiled. She is smiling?

If only she'd been stronger. She might have lived. They said she was a fighter – fought to the last. 'You should have seen her when she was young,' he thought – 'Fight? fight? Had more spirit than most men . . . like the time when she'd gone out and slammed the door. Thought she'd gone for good. It was such a row: and afterwards I felt terrible. But she'd come back – still fighting. Marvellous. I loved her. . .'

The lump in his throat. The empty ache in his chest. It was unbearable. The door bell rang. His daughter answered it. 'It's Gail and Andrew, Dad,' she called. His young grand-daughter and her husband. All of life before them.

27

'Hello, Grandad,' Gail's eyes brimmed with tears as she bent to kiss him. He loved her too. Very like her grandmother. Same eyes. He hugged her – a bit clumsily. Shook hands with Andrew.

'I suppose it's all for the best,' he said to Gail – and looked out of the window again. The tears were welling up. 'Lord: it's all for the best, isn't it? I mean if she'd gone on living it would have been a real struggle. And you'll look after her for me, won't you? And tell her "I'll see her," that's all, "I'll see her." '

'Dad, you'll need your coat. It's time to go. . .'

God replies:

My loving child, of course I will. Of course I will. Remember that I love you. I love her.

My love is boundless and eternal: it reaches across death like a bridge, spanning heaven and earth, and upon that bridge you, in your turn, will one day walk.

And 'all for the best?' you ask. The question is fair and true. In very truth, in the light of eternity all is for the best – when goodness and love and truth and beauty and glory will dance, dance for sheer joy. At the end of a life on earth, a full life, a rounded life, you can see that it's 'all for the best' – but I know that in sudden death, in the death of a child, to talk of 'all for the best' seems a blasphemy. What then? What shall you think then?

I do not *will* the death of children; I do not *will* accidents; I do not *will* disaster. But remember me then by the name 'Redeemer': for I shall be with you even in the darkest hour and out of that darkness light will come.

Remember me then as 'servant', as one 'despised and rejected' who shares the desolation with you. There is no depth you can plummet that is beyond me: at rock bottom there is rock.

Remember me then as 'Saviour' – being with you to save you from despair, from the abyss.

'My will is done on earth as in heaven' where justice replaces injustice; where reconciliation replaces hatred; where mercy is shown to the weak and forgiveness to the sinful.

My will is done on earth when my love is let loose within you and among you and around you.

My will is done on earth when through it all you trust me.

Am I not your Father?
Am I not your Lord?
Am I not your brother, your sister, your mother?

Give us this day our daily bread . . .

'I can only find one sock.' He's the youngest, who has come hopping into the kitchen on a Monday morning, hair crumpled, tie awry, shirt-tail sticking out. 'Mum: do you know where my sock is?'

The eldest (by two years) sighs with exasperation: 'Have you looked in the drawer?'

'Which drawer?'

'There *is* only one drawer with your socks in.'

'Oh.' He turns away and hops out of the room.

'Hurry up: your breakfast's waiting.' At the window the cat miaows to be fed. Brian Redhead and another presenter share banter on the 'Today' programme. Mother, meanwhile, is making coffee and toast. The eldest eats cornflakes noisily and seems intent on reading every single word on the packet: 'Mum, what's Niacin?'

'There's delay on most Southern region trains into Waterloo this morning,' announces the radio. Father enters:

'What did they say?'

'The trains are running late. . .' It's said quietly and placatingly to prevent a volcanic eruption. He glowers. Pours some muesli. Drinks his coffee. Grunts at the eldest. Enquires after the whereabouts of the youngest. (The cat is still miaowing.)

'Mum,' the voice is distant, 'which drawer did you say?'

The eldest sighs again. 'He forgot his tie yesterday.' (There's nothing like crowing over the failures of the youngest.)

'Yes: well, you're not so brilliant yourself.'

A ring at the door bell. 'Go and see who that is.'

Another sigh as the cornflakes are pushed aside. 'The postman,' he calls out. 'Shall I sign for it?' 'Yes.'

The toast has reached the stage known in the trade as 'bien cuit'.

'Can I borrow a sock?'

The post is brought in: an ominous collection of manilla envelopes with cellophane windows.

The cat has given up miaowing but now scratches at the door.

'I just don't know how I'm going to get through today.' Father has spoken his first words.

Mother nods. 'Nor me.' She is opening the envelopes. 'I've got to be out of here by a quarter-to-eight,' she says.

The eldest asks, 'What's Riboflavin?'

The youngest hops back into the room. 'Is my PE kit washed?'

He continues to hop. He now has both socks on, but only one shoe. Father is not reading the paper; he's demolishing it. 'If I were Chancellor . . .' Mother, already running the washing-up water, prays:

'Lord: give us this day our daily bread
— a ration of patience
— a ration of wisdom
— a dose of good humour (and no more bills)
— and please may I remember to take something out of the freezer for tonight . . .

(Anyone seen my shoes?') . . .

'In fact, Lord, just help me survive, get through the day intact – and bless this lot.

('Anyone know where the car keys are?')

'– bless them with their share of "bread": safety, kindness, good health – and, Lord, remind me of your presence in the rush and give us all peace for Jesus' sake.'

God replies:

Yes.

It's as simple as that. Yes. I try to get my 'Yes' across to you: for you to see that my 'Yes' to you *is* your daily bread. Remember 'I am the bread of life'. At the very centre of your being I feed you: I nourish you with my Being: coming to you in love and great power.

Remember, 'Take, eat, this is my body.' Do I not continue to feed your soul? Do I not give myself to you in the bread of the Eucharist – meeting your needs, strengthening you in body, mind and spirit for the day?

Remember, 'Man shall not live by bread alone' – and in your daily life make room for that which is 'not bread'. Give space for music: give space for laughter and friendship: give space for silence: give space for me.

Remember, 'When did we see you hungry?': and in your life share your bread with those who starve – in mind, body or soul. You *are* your brother's keeper.

Remember, 'How many loaves are there?' I shall feed you no matter how small your offering – and give thanks, take, break and bless with you.

Remember the Emmaus road: for when you share your 'bread', there am I.

Lord, give us this day our daily bread.

Forgive us our trespasses . . .

Everyman speaks:

'Well, have you heard? . . . Look, if I tell you, you promise you won't tell a soul . . . oh, I don't know if I should . . . anyway . . . no, I don't think I shall . . . but . . . no names. OK? No names.

'You know that new car they've got . . . and the house. Have you seen the house? Gutted. Top to bottom. New carpets, curtains, the finest interior decorator they could lay hands on. . . It's a palace – not a home, of course, not a home. Not a thing out of place. So immaculate even the goldfish are polished.

'Mind you, they do say that car number plate should read "TD 1". TD 1? Tax Dodge, dear. Tax dodge. I admire it really: if you pay, it only goes to the scroungers, doesn't it?

'On the telly the other night there was this unemployed man. Not prepared to go anywhere. They deserve it. Honest they do – I mean if they won't work they shouldn't eat, should they? They make me so mad.

'Which reminds me – we went to this fantastic place for a meal the other day. Sumptuous – and a gorgeous waiter. Narrow hips. You know the sort. You could eat him. . . And they had these quails' eggs. My dear – they must have cost a fortune. If I ate one I ate a dozen. No, I don't know what it cost. *He* paid. The old man – firm's cheque book – and afterwards we went back to their place for drinks. . .

'I'm not jealous by nature, you know I'm not – but if you'd seen the coat she was wearing. And she threw it down as casually as though she'd got it from an Oxfam shop – but she made sure I saw the label. Clever, wasn't it?

'But I showed her up later, you know. Told her about the company – not straight out of course. Just hints. Dropped a few names: Rio, Tokyo, Gstaad, Acapulco, Copacabana – you know, just to make sure they know. . . It was a good evening. Got back late. Slept like a log. Woke about ten and sort of mooned around. Painted my nails. Ordered a bit of shopping (isn't it hopeless getting things delivered?) and before I knew where I was it was lunch time.

'Then after lunch all hell broke loose. I'd ordered this new table. Sweet little thing really – and when they brought it in I saw a mark on one of the legs. I said to the man: "Look at that – look what you've done." He was so rude. I mean, he denied it. "No I didn't," he said. Well, if there's one thing I can't stand it's that sort of insolence. I gave him a piece of my mind . . . and he answered back with such a mouthful, so I told him to take it away. I phoned the shop, spoke to the manager; said I'd never, *never* go there again and what is more I should tell all my friends. And that's that. And I shan't change. No, my dear. Once my mind's made up that's it. Finish . . . well, I don't think you should. It's a sign of weakness and I'm not weak. My mind shall not be changed. . .

'So, Lord, thank you for everything I have . . . and thank you for, well, you know . . . it's worked out all right really. . .'

God replies:

My child . . . all my children, if only you could count.

I don't wish to appear old-fashioned but when I last looked I remember 'seven deadly sins' . . . pride, lust, covetousness, envy, greed, anger, sloth. . .

Now I admit that once you start cataloguing sins you have a field day . . . if you're proud that you're not greedy, for example . . . that's a real spiral – downwards.

But to be honest (I can't be otherwise, can I? Go on: smile) . . . it's not the seven deadly sins which bother me most. Don't be surprised . . . no, not seven sins or even seventy-seven. What breaks my heart is when you fail to forgive. Deliberately, wilfully, viciously failing to forgive: that is the end.

And there is a law in my kingdom: a law in my world. If you do not forgive, you will not be forgiven . . . simple, straightforward and to the point. You see, forgiveness is not a matter of intelligence or learning or technique . . . it's a matter of your will. You can choose to forgive. Every human being has that capacity. Nothing can stop you forgiving except yourself.

So: if there's a note of warning in my voice, heed it. Heed it.

You are free to forgive others. Nothing can prevent you . . . and if you choose *not* to forgive, you will not be in a state to receive my forgiveness. It's as simple as that.

Remember: 'Do not condemn others and you will not be condemned: forgive others and God will forgive you. . .'

Remember the story of the speck of sawdust and the plank?

Remember the Pharisee and the tax collector?

So: be forgiving with all your heart: forgive and you will be forgiven . . . and in forgiveness you will discover a generosity which will transform everything . . . but fail to forgive and, well, you'll become narrow and hard and mean and dead: inside.

For the sake of love, forgive – and whilst you're about it don't forget to forgive yourself; that's sometimes the hardest of all.

Father, forgive us our trespasses as we forgive those who trespass against us.

Lead us not into temptation, but deliver us from evil

Everyman speaks:

Look, Lord: the time has come to take the gloves off. Perhaps I can explain?

I have an instinctive feeling that I'm about to enter into very dangerous and difficult territory, but I shall have to be honest before venturing in. That's what I mean about getting the gloves off. I'll come straight to the point. It's this: 'lead us not into temptation'; who is doing the 'leading'?

If I ask you in this prayer not to lead me into temptation, I'm implying that temptation could be your affair. That's difficult. Very difficult. I've looked through the Bible – and confusion is worse confounded.

I turn to dear old Jacob: wrestling Jacob. You remember – the one who dreamt of ladders. A kind of heavenly window-cleaner. And what do I find? He wrestled – but with whom? With an angel? With the Adversary? With you? If it was with you – and it looks as though it was – why disjoint him? He limped from the ordeal.

So I turn from that to Jesus: and, forgive me, but it's not terribly, terribly clear – if you know what I mean. I see that he was tempted in the wilderness – but here's the bit which dismays me (may I take the liberty of reminding you?): 'He was led by the Spirit into the wilderness. . .'

So: you see why I'm bothered. If it was just the Adversary who led him into the wilderness to be tempted, that at least would be understandable. But when I discover that it's you (after all, the prayer doesn't beat about the bush, does it?) – what am I to think?

I'll keep on this track of thinking, if I may – because, awe-ful though it is, those images of wrestling, limping Jacob and Jesus going out into the wilderness have a truth about them deeper than words.

I realise, Lord, that temptation doesn't just mean nicking pencils from work, or gloating over some magazine, or thinking gossipy, cruel thoughts: it's far bigger than that. It's about 'trial'. I know that.

'Do not bring me to the time of trial.' I can pray that with all my heart – because cowardice could be my middle name. But suppose it's you – you, Lord, leading me to that trial. What then? Shall I be disjointed with the struggle? Shall I sweat like our Lord at Gethsemane?

I can understand the pain and the agony because at that point I am in the darkness – a darkness which seems to be marked by your presence.

Lord, if you lead me to that kind of test, shall I cope? Do I have to accept that even there you are? Do I have to obey even whilst I scream a 'No'? And the thing is, Lord: in England in this part of the twentieth century the 'trial' is unlikely to be public; the wilderness I know is not outside but inside. Will you lead me even there to be tested? And if you do – shall I hang on in there in the faith that somewhere, in the silent screaming, you are? Lord: I can pray with all my heart 'Lead me not into that trial. . .'

'And deliver me from evil': Oh yes. Oh yes – preserve me from evil: from the hollow emptiness of evil: from the abyss, from the terror of not-being, from the wiles and dupes, the snares and traps – from all that: good Lord deliver me . . . I can pray that most fervently – but if my prayer to you is touched with fear of the test, will you understand?

As I said: the gloves were off. I've tried to be as straight as I can – but that limping Jacob haunts me. . .

God replies:

My loving child, let me straighten you out on one thing to begin with: you have prayed 'Lead me not into temptation: deliver me from evil . . .' I understand – but can't you see that the prayer says 'us'? You aren't in this alone – to think that you are is egocentric. The prayer says 'us'. You and your friends, your brothers and sisters in Christ pray that together. The 'trial' is for you – communally. Being delivered from evil is for you – communally. Please don't forget that – otherwise you become a bunch of individuals writing spiritual temperature charts for yourselves, and comparing one with another.

Do you think you might be the only one being tested? Do you think you are the only one praying for deliverance? Every single one of your brothers and sisters is tested. Every one. You are not alone.

So: off your egocentric bike, my child, and get on the coach with the rest. But now to try to answer your questions. I'm not certain I like being interviewed: however. . .

Of course the Spirit is there in the trial. Please believe that. Be comforted by that. And why the trial? If you are to grow, do you not need challenge? If you are to come close to me, do you think you can do so instantly and blandly? (You've got me asking questions now. . .). The trial will be to the edge of your limits – and what is trial for you may not be trial for others . . . and why to the edge? Because there you are, at the growing edge.

As for the wilderness. Yes: in your life, in your part of the world, the wilderness is within . . . full of wild beasts. But do you suppose that that is beyond my reach and my love? Could it be that that is what I desire for you – in my wisdom and understanding?

The pain is real. As real as the silent scream – I do not deny that. But only the wounded surgeon knows the cost of healing. Do you think that the wounds are not mine?

So: my child: I am with you. There is no place you can go, no depths you can plummet, that I am not there. In your trials I shall be there alongside you . . . and I shall deliver you from evil – for I share with you my kingdom, my power and my glory, now and for ever. . .

The Beatitudes

Tell it slant/success in circuit lies.

(*Emily Dickinson*)

Stanley Spencer continued a long artistic tradition when he painted Christ and the disciples as inhabitants of a Thames-side village. In writing the same risk has not often been taken. In the meditations which follow, the disciples and Jesus are pictured as living in a leafy Surrey 'village' – well, why not? – and the conversations they have are, I hope, both true to the original thrust of the Beatitudes and yet also with a twentieth-century ring.

Blessed are the poor in spirit

'We're all catching the 9.32 to get a Cheap Day Return.' Peter, being the Chairman of the group, has got it all organised. 'Then once we get to Waterloo we shall hold our meeting in the park in front of the Shell building.'

It is a fine spring day, warm and mellow. A day for a picnic, the first of the year. We pile on to the train, talk non-stop all the way there and find that the carriage is very, very full.

'Crowded,' says Peter in his usual insightful way.

At Waterloo we are disgorged, walk through the concourse; 'I want a hamburger,' says Matthew, but he's reminded that that would be against the Law . . . and out across the road-bridge, the traffic swirling beneath us – through the Shell building, down the steps and into the South Bank park.

'This seems a good spot,' someone says, and we all sit down. Jesus, looking at the crowds that have gathered, decides to sit in the bandstand – and then calls us out from the crowd.

'They can listen,' he says, 'but what I have to say is to you – the disciples – the crowd can eavesdrop.'

We look at each other, afraid? bewildered? delighted that we have been chosen, separated out? . . . Jesus begins.

He looks at us all very closely – looking at each one of us in turn. His eyes are filled with a sad compassion. We wait.

The silence as we wait grows deeper. He starts: 'Blessed are the poor in spirit: the kingdom of heaven is theirs. . .'

And that's all. That's all he says. He looks at us – waiting for questions. Peter, thank goodness, asks the first: 'Lord, what does "poor in spirit" mean?' Good old Peter – he's always willing to ask what the rest of us only think.

Jesus replies: 'See that man over there, the one rummaging through the litter – he's poor. Really, really poor. He has to beg. He isn't just poor in relation to the rich . . . that man has nothing. Nothing. He is reduced to begging.'

'Being poor in spirit is being like that – only inside your very soul. . .'

We all look at the ground. A seagull glides past and on the other side of the park a group of black schoolchildren walk past with their teachers.

41

The crowds are listening now:

'When I got on the train at Farnham,' said Jesus, 'with all of you, I could see that there is not one of you who is materially poor: not one. . .'

We mentally count the number of credit cards we have in our wallets – and remember the names of our bank managers.

'Not one of you is poor,' said Jesus. 'I say to you "Blessed are the poor in spirit: for theirs is the kingdom of heaven". . .' He waits again for our response: we shift uneasily.

'You aren't poor: but you need to be if you are to discover the kingdom of God: poor in your very soul. . .'

'Lord,' says Thomas, 'forgive me, but what do you mean?'

Jesus smiled and sighed at one and the same time. . .

'The great problem for you,' he said, 'is that you can compensate for your poverty of spirit by your purchasing power . . . but, Thomas, have you never felt, deep inside, at your wits' end? Like looking over an abyss? – as though the ground itself is opening up? Have you never felt the exhaustion, the terror of your own poverty – when suddenly, like a shaft of lightning, you see, you experience the utter poverty of your very self?'

Thomas tries to avoid the question. 'Lord . . .' he begins, 'Lord . . . you know I have.'

The other disciples look astonished. They begin to speak to him. 'But we thought you had it made.' 'We thought you had it comfortable, Thomas, that you had everything you wanted. . .' 'You always seemed so happy. . .'

42

Jesus looks at Thomas.

'I may have,' he said, 'but I do know that most of the time I don't know at all. I just don't know . . . I don't suppose any one of you feels like that. . .'

'Rubbish,' said Peter. The others agreed.

' "Blessed are the poor in spirit",' said Jesus, looking straight at Thomas, 'for only when you accept the poverty and the loneliness of your inmost being – only then are you close to God. . .'

'Why?'

'You know why,' said Jesus. 'Because then, and only then, do you turn to God and say, "Help me." You come to him in your nakedness, like a beggar – and he says "Yes . . . you are loved".'

'So when I am almost screaming inside,' said Thomas, 'screaming with loneliness and fear . . . then I am near the kingdom of heaven?'

'Right,' said Jesus. 'On the very threshold. . .'

'And that is blessed?'

'Yes' said Jesus, 'because you are held by God. You trust in him. . .'

'There could be quite a few of us like me,' said Thomas. 'God can cope, can he?'

'Absolutely,' said Jesus. 'Especially if you can share your inner poverty with each other. . .'

43

'Ah,' said Thomas: 'that's not a catch, is it?'

'No,' said Jesus, 'it's the truth.'

Blessed are they that mourn

'The rendezvous is different this time,' he said. 'We're going for a walk.'

'Can I go back for my trainers?' asked Matthew. 'My sandals have holes in them.'

They waited, talking about this and that, and admired the hard work of the gardeners in the churchyard. 'Pity about the cedar,' said someone. 'Did you "cedar" fall?' asked Peter – but no-one saw the joke.

Matthew came panting through the churchyard and the walk got under way. Down Old Church Lane and into Dene Lane, up into The Bourne woods, out to Tilford, stopping at 'The Barley Mow' for refreshments. ('Take Courage,' said Peter.) Then left along a path and eventually through the woods until he said, 'We stop here.'

It was an enchanting place, carpeted with snowdrops, over-looking the river and in sight of the ruins of Waverley Abbey.

Quietness descended on the disciples – an expectant silence. Jesus had his back to them, looking out over the river. Above the ruins of the Abbey a hawk was hovering. They all waited. Jesus turned and spoke:

'Blessed are they that mourn: they shall be comforted.'

Thomas coughed, apologised and said, 'Could you please say that again. I want to think about it some more.'

At that moment the hawk dived.

'Blessed are they that mourn: they shall be comforted.'

It was a strange, an ominous remark – did it look back to the losses the disciples themselves had suffered? Parents? Children? Or forward to the unknown? It touched a few very tender scars. Peter coloured slightly – and looked at Jesus with his lovely, innocent eyes.

'Lord,' he said, 'Why did you say that to us?' Jesus turned, looking again towards the ruins.

'Peter the rock,' he replied – and saw the crumbling buttresses, the broken windows. 'What have you suffered? What will you suffer for my sake?'

The disciples waited for Peter's reply.

'I have left a lot of things behind,' said Peter. . . 'Family, friends, brothers, village. . .'

'And you miss them?'

'Sometimes,' he said, 'terribly.'

'Blessed are those who mourn. . .'

'To be honest, Lord, it doesn't often feel very blessed. It's more like desolation.'

'Peter,' said Jesus, 'Only those who love can know what desolation is . . . and only those who are desolate know the *power* of love, and the healing grace of the Holy Spirit, the Comforter.'

'Blessed are those who mourn: they shall be comforted.'

'In your desolation,' continued Jesus, 'God your Heavenly Father supports you. . . "Underneath are the everlasting arms." No matter what happens there is no situation which is beyond the grace and mercy and love of our Father. . . "If I climb up into heaven, you are there: if I go down to hell you are there also".'

The disciples were very still. In the warmth of the spring afternoon a few midges were dancing over the surface of the river. Overhead some geese in a V-formation flew with a resolute and beautiful purpose. They seemed so strong.

'Your past,' said Jesus looking up at the geese, 'is also in the hands of God . . . and when you mourn your past offer that too to God for he is there, beyond time – "and you shall be comforted" '.

Matthew was heartened by that. He carried around with him guilt about his past, his shady dealings. Simon thought of his desire to stick a zealot's knife between the shoulder-blades of a Roman. James and John remembered all those times when their tempers had flared – hot and dangerous as lightning. All those people they had hurt . . . all those people, perhaps some dead, to whom they could not say 'Sorry'. Living with that weight, mourning the missed opportunities.

Thomas picked up a stick and swished at a few leaves – disturbing some woodlice and a delicate spider. They scuttled into the safety of a tree root.

'Blessed are those who mourn,' said Jesus, 'they shall be strengthened.' (It was another shade of meaning of 'comforted.') 'Strengthened?' asked Thomas. 'I can understand "comfort" but "strength"?'

'Have you never watched a blacksmith at work, Thomas? Have you never seen him heat the metal in the fire, work upon it and only when he is satisfied does he plunge the red-hot iron into water. Have you never seen that?'

'Yes, Lord, I have.'

'And is the iron not stronger when he has finished?'

'Yes, Lord. . .'

'Well, dear Thomas,' said Jesus 'your mourning is not unlike that. You are plunged into grief, like iron into water. If you allow yourself to be held by God, He will strengthen you.'

'James and John,' he said, addressing the brothers. 'You are hot-tempered. Will you allow yourselves to be "tempered" by God?'

'Yes, Lord . . . you know we will.'

'Simon the zealot: man of steel – will you be "steeled" by God?'

'Yes Lord, you know I will. . .'

He looked around at the other disciples, his eyes resting on each one of them in turn. They waited:

'. . . and the Son of Man,' he said, 'will be delivered to the chief priests and the scribes, and they will condemn him to death, and deliver him to the Gentiles: and they will mock him, and spit upon him and scourge him and kill him – and after three days he will rise.'

They were still silent. He held out his hands towards them: 'Blessed are those who mourn: they shall be comforted.'

The disciples looked at each other and then out over the river. The hawk had resumed his hovering above the ruins of the Abbey – but somewhere in the bushes nearby a robin began to sing.

Blessed are the meek

'Do you accept cash?' asked Peter. 'Only I don't have a credit card.'

'Indeed, sir,' said the girl at the desk, 'but we shall need a driving licence and insurance certificate.' Peter fumbled around in his sports jacket pockets and pulled out train tickets, sweet papers and a Marks and Spencer receipt ('Support the home firm,' he said.) He passed over his insurance certificate. 'Ecclesiastical Insurance Company,' he said. 'Safe as a rock.' He smiled to himself.

'Are you going far, sir?'

'No, just out for a drive with some friends.' The paper-work completed, she showed him to a Ford Transit mini-bus. 'Seats 12,' she said.

'Ideal,' said Peter.

He started it up, let the clutch out too quickly and stalled.

'They're usually easy to drive,' she said. Peter was not amused. He lurched out of the station yard around the front of the forecourt where they were all waiting.

'Pile in,' he said.

'Who are we playing?' asked Thaddaeus. Matthew asked if the van was taxed. James and John began to sing songs: 'Oh you'll never go to heaven in a Transit van. . .'

They drove out into the country and stopped on a ridge of high land near Well. The view across the valley to Alice Holt was lovely and in the faint blue distance they could see the hills around Hindhead.

They got out, stretched, walked down a bridleway and stopped in a field marked by ridges and humps. 'The OS map,' said Peter, 'says it's the site of old Roman iron workings.'

He stood with his back to a tree. Beyond him the valley, with the light washing across the purple clumps of birch-trees in spring bud. Somehow he had the ability to create stillness. They pocketed their Mars Bar wrappers and waited.

'Blessed are the meek,' said Jesus, 'for they shall inherit the earth.'

Above his head the branches of the tree were just beginning to break into bud. A blackbird sang boldly from a nearby hedge.

'You,' he said, looking around at them all, 'you shall inherit the earth.'

'We can't even afford our own van,' said Philip, 'so how are we going to inherit the earth?'

'If you are meek,' said Jesus, 'and lowly of heart: you shall inherit the earth.' They waited. He went on:

'You will listen, O God, to the prayers of the lowly; you will give them courage.'

'But who are the meek?' Philip persisted with his question.

'The meek,' said Jesus, 'are children playing in a recreation ground; the meek are old and ancient gardeners who tend flowers with huge chapped hands; the meek are those facing death: no longer in control, they are themselves controlled and in their poverty discover inner strength.'

'And the children in the playground?'

'They have no rights, no money of their own, no say in their future – but they experience a joy lost to most of us.'

'And the gardeners?'

'They know what patience is – and the miracle of re-birth. They don't "make" gardens, they go with the grain of the garden and accept the life which is not theirs. . .'

'The meek,' he said, 'are those who abandon their lives to God – like children abandon themselves to happiness, or gardeners to their task, or the dying to an unknown future . . . if you abandon your very soul to God you will learn meekness. . .'

They looked back at him and thought of his days in the desert: his battles with evil.

'Take up your cross,' he said, 'and follow me. . . Whoever would seek to save his life will lose it, but whoever loses his life for me and the gospel will save it.'

The shadow of the tree fell across their faces. They were very still. 'Blessed are the meek,' he said, 'for they shall inherit the earth.'

Judas looked very troubled. 'How can they, Lord?' he asked. 'It's only by the exercise of political power that the poor will get justice. Come the revolution. . .'

'Agreed,' said James and John, 'and we'll be there with you, Lord, sorting them all out.'

'I know that that is the way of the world,' said Jesus, 'but amongst you the greatest must be like the youngest, and the leader must be like the servant. I am among you,' he continued, 'as one who serves.

'Blessed are the meek: for they shall inherit the earth. Why? How? Because the earth is God's.

'He loves the lowly – for they and they alone have the eyes to see. Nothing gets in the way of their vision.

'They and they alone can hear the glory of God in the world: nothing gets in the way of their hearing.

'They and they alone, in their quietness and patience, in the acknowledgment of their poverty – they alone know the boundless grace of God. . .

'Where your treasure is, there will your heart be also. . .

'Place your heart in the hands of God and you will learn meekness,' he said, 'and when you do you shall inherit the earth.'

'It's time we moved on,' he said. 'I suggest "The Chequers", agreed?'

'Aye,' they said.

But who was it who asked, 'Who pays the bill?'

Blessed are the merciful

The weather was mild and as they passed the old churchyard they saw primroses tucked up against gravestones. A few daffodils danced in the breeze.

'Where's Peter?' asked Matthew.

'Gone to see a man about a dog,' said Philip.

'He went to the dogs years ago.'

'Should have stuck to fishing.'

At the corner of Vicarage Hill and Swingate Road they stopped. Peter was hurtling along the road, towed by a dalmatian at full speed.

'Oh, look: he's caught a pup. . .'

'And it's Rocky on the outside rails coming up fast but making little headway. . .' It was Thaddaeus who began his imitation of a racing commentator. 'And Rocky appears to be swaying a little. Yes, he's definitely cracked up: he's slowing right down. Has he pulled a tendon? Will he be seen by the vet?'

'It's all very well for you,' said Peter, gasping for breath, 'you lot would go for a walk any day and never think to bring a friend.'.'.

'It's a dog's life, Peter.' 'Don't hound us, Pete.' 'Oh, leave him alone, his bark's worse than his bite. . .'

The young dalmatian, called Nona, wagged her tail and licked everyone.

The walk was well and truly under way. Down Vicarage Hill, across the Tilford Road and into Boreas Dene. Some horses were grazing quietly in the meadow. They turned, looked and walked towards the disciples. Peter attempted to converse with one of them by saying, 'Neigh.'

'Let your yea be yea and your neigh be neigh,' said someone.

Nona, let off the lead in another meadow, sped across the grass. They all watched her.

'Isn't that beautiful? That's freedom.'

Jesus looked at Nona running: 'Blessed are the merciful,' he said. 'For they shall obtain mercy.'

'Ah,' said Peter after a short pause. 'Ah . . . Sorry, but I don't see what mercy has to do with a dog.'

Jesus smiled. 'Somebody mentioned "freedom",' he said, 'and when you see Nona run you can see the joy of freedom.

She rejoices. She exults in the space, the springy turf. Let off the lead she is a kind of alleluia – running . . . and mercy is like that. Mercy freely given conveys freedom and a joy beyond words. . .'

'Thank you,' said Peter. 'I think I understand: it's Nona's joy in running which gives us joy in watching.'

'Spot on,' said Jesus. Peter winced at the dalmatian pun.

'And mercy may be joyful,' said Matthew, 'but what is it in itself?'

' "Thy mercy, O Lord, reacheth unto the heavens: and thy faithfulness unto the clouds." Mercy,' said Jesus, 'is the heart of God. It is the life of God winging through the Universe with a joy unfettered. It is the kindness, the loyal, generous kindness of a steadfast man: that's what mercy is . . . and those who give that sort of steadfast love to others are given it in return.'

Nona came trotting back into the circle of the disciples. She leapt up at Peter and licked him.

'See,' said Jesus, 'her joy is only really complete when it's shared with you . . . and is not God the same? His mercy is completed when you yourselves are merciful. "And what does the Lord require of you but to do justice, and to love kindness and to walk humbly with your God?" '

They began to walk again, following the route of the old Pilgrims' Way. 'The pilgrims always told stories, didn't they?' asked Thomas. 'I vote that we tell stories as we walk.'

'Agreed,' they said. Jesus began: 'There was once a man who had two sons, and the younger of them said to his father,

54

"Father, give me the share of the property that belongs to me. . ." '

They waited by a stile on the edge of the wood while Jesus rounded off the story. Nona went snuffling through the leaves in search of rabbits. 'Blessed are the merciful,' said Jesus, at the end of the story of the Prodigal Son, 'for they shall obtain mercy.'

Peter repeated the words to himself. 'Blessed are the merciful. . .' He called Nona. She returned and stood a few feet off, looking at him with puzzled eyes.

'She thinks you're talking to her,' said Philip. 'Stop muttering, Peter, and give her a hug.'

'I was only learning my lines,' said Peter. He bent down, rubbed Nona's head and back. 'There,' he said. 'Now I know what mercy is.'

At that moment Nona tugged on her lead. Peter, off balance, stumbled and tore his coat on the barbed wire fence. 'That was my best jacket,' he said furiously.

'Remember your lines,' said Thomas.

'Thank you very much,' he replied, with a degree of hurt feeling. 'You didn't doubt me, did you, Tom?'

Thomas did not reply.

Jesus looked round at them all. 'When I'm gone,' he said, 'be merciful as your heavenly Father is merciful . . . and especially, be merciful to each other.' It sounded like a command.

They waited for him to explain. Instead he climbed the stile and strode out along the Pilgrims' Way on his own. The disciples all made a rush for the stile at once and in the middle of them Nona barked and licked them and bounced with happiness.

'After you,' said Peter, who was last in the queue, to Thomas. Thomas only grinned. He waited for Peter to haul himself over and then said, 'Haven't you forgotten Nona's lead?'

'Oh, blow,' said Peter, preparing to climb back over the stile. 'You might have told me.'

And when he was straddled halfway across, Thomas called, 'Look!' and held up Nona's lead in his hand. Peter was not amused.

'Blessed are the merciful,' said Thomas. 'Remember?'

Blessed are those who hunger and thirst after righteousness

It was the day of the parish walk. Cars drove into the churchyard, passengers were picked up, doors slammed, engines revved and they were off.

This time Peter was a passenger. 'Where are we going?' 'We have an OS reference point,' said the driver. 'Can you read a map?' 'I should say,' replied Peter. 'Turn left along the Ridgway Road,' he said, 'and on out to the Petersfield road.'

He did very well until they actually got to South Harting, and then the trouble started. 'Somewhere,' he said, 'there should be a car park.' It was a statement of the obvious. The other passengers said nothing. 'I'm sure if we took this turning.' The driver indicated a left turn. 'Or perhaps not . . .' The car behind hooted. 'I expect that's James or John,' he said. 'Thundering nuisance they can be.'

After much to-ing and fro-ing and many three-point turns, they eventually made the car park. Everyone else was already there. There were cheers as Peter stepped out. . .

'Sorry,' he said, 'but I think our map must have been wrong.' 'You look "keyed" up,' said someone. 'I "contour" what you're saying,' replied Peter. He was unabashed.

It was a baking hot day, not a cloud in the sky, the grass brown and brittle beneath their feet.

The walk began. It was a cracking pace. Faces became redder and redder. Conversations which began sparkingly soon were reduced to monosyllabic grunts. The heat as they walked through a cornfield was intense. No-one had remembered to bring a drink.

They came to the edge of a copse and threw themselves down in the shade – but even that was warm. The grass was so dry that sucking it brought no juices.

'I'm dying for a drink,' said Peter. The others only had the energy to nod. Flies were pestering them, playing around their ears and foreheads. 'Where's the nearest pub?' 'Miles away.'

And then Jesus spoke. He was reclining in the shade. 'Blessed are those who hunger and thirst after righteousness,' he said, 'for they shall be satisfied.'

'Please don't talk about thirst,' said Matthew, 'I'm parched. Dry as a bone. My mouth's like a desert.' The others nodded.

'Are you thirsty?' asked Jesus.

'Lord, I am desperate for a drink,' said Thomas.

'And do you thirst as much for righteousness,' asked Jesus, 'as you do for water? Really thirst, I mean. Longing with all your heart to quench your desire. . .'

'All I want right now,' said Thomas, 'is a long cool drink.'

'But is your desire for righteousness as strong as your desire for water?'

'What kind of righteousness, Lord?'

'Do you thirst for a righteous and just society? Where there is no torture, no crucifixion, no poverty, no disease. Do you thirst for that?

'Do you thirst for a righteous heart for yourself – to live totally within the will of God?

'Do you thirst for the cause to prevail in which you believe? Do you thirst for that?'

In the heat over the Downs larks were rising. Their song pierced the silence with a joy too intense for words. They all listened, centring on the song.

'To be honest, Lord,' said Peter, I don't think I thirst as much for those things as I do for a drink now.'

'But you want righteousness, don't you?' asked Jesus. 'Righteousness in society? in your own heart? for me?'

'Yes, Lord . . . you know I do.'

'Well then, beloved Peter – you are on the way. . .'

('Don't ask him to map-read, though,' said James.)

'How do you mean, Lord?' said Peter.

'It is not the perfect man that God requires – not the complete and integrated man. That perfection can only come the other side of the grave. You may not thirst for righteousness totally – but within your heart you long to do something for God. . .'

'Yes, Lord. . .'

'That,' said Jesus, 'is the beginning of thirst, and it is a thirst which will grow and grow. . . "Like as the hart desireth the water brooks. . .".'

'But that kind of thirst is painful, Lord. It hurts my soul. I yearn for God. I long for his comforting presence, for holiness. . .'

'Since when,' asked Jesus, 'has the way to God been easy? But each day God will give you sufficient nourishment for your soul . . . each day. No more. No less.

'Meanwhile, your longing, your dissatisfaction, your thirst, is a sign from God to you. He says: "You are on the right track. Seek and you shall find. . . And I shall give unto him that is athirst of the fountain of life freely and he that over-

59

cometh shall inherit all things and I will be his God and he shall be my Son. . ."

'It's time we were on our way,' he said. 'Ready?'

But some were more ready to begin than others. . .

Blessed are the pure in heart

'We are off to see Pompey,' he said.

'I can't stand the Romans,' said Simon.

'Not the General,' replied Peter, 'Don't be crazy – we're going to Portsmouth for the day.' All the sailors in the party cheered; the rest seemed faintly glum.

The coach pulled out of the churchyard, packed to the gunwales. Peter was in charge. 'No singing; no stamping; no whistling,' he said. 'No fun,' said Thomas. He was in a gloomy, doubting sort of mood.

Just before Petersfield Peter stood up and announced that they all ought to keep a respectful silence as they drove through the town. 'They know a good name when they see one,' he said. The disciples on the back seat booed.

At Portsmouth they all piled out on to the quay. 'I've forgotten my bucket and spade,' said Philip.

'Can we go for a swim?' – and someone began to croon: 'Gone fishing.'

They walked through the dockyard gates following the signs to HMS *Victory*, and queued with the hundreds of school-children and day-trippers in trilbys and white cardigans. A Royal Marine greeted their party: 'Welcome on board, ladies and gentlemen. The *Victory*, as you will know, was the flagship of Lord Nelson.'

'Who was he?' whispered Peter.

'A kind of English Zebedee,' said James and John, remembering the sailing exploits of their father.

The tour began and they looked in wonder at cannons and cats-of-nine-tails and felt sorry for the 'powder monkeys'. On the surgeon's deck, painted red so that the blood would not show ('The surgeon could amputate a leg in 90 seconds; an arm in 45 seconds; and a finger in nine,' said the guide) a few of them felt queasy. It was only when they reached the main deck and felt the sea-air on their faces that they revived.

'Blest are the pure in heart,' whispered Jesus to Peter. Peter was running his hands enviously along the newly painted and elegant lines of the longboat. 'But you have to admit it's a nice boat, Lord.' Matthew had detached himself slightly from the rest of them and was talking to a pretty girl from Manchester. Peter sidled up to him, 'Blest are the pure in heart,' he said 'Pass it on.' James, meanwhile, was looking at a very large American carrying an expensive and beautiful camera. Matthew tapped him on the shoulder, 'Blest are the pure in heart,' he said, 'Pass it on.'

The tour over, they shambled down the gangplank and on to the quay. Jesus, stationing himself next to a figure-head of Nelson, and drinking from a can of Coke, waited. They gathered around.

'He put the telescope to his blind eye,' said Jesus about Nelson, 'and said "I see no ships".'

It was, even by his standards, an elliptical remark. Peter was bothered. He liked things straight, 'ship-shape and Bristol fashion'.

'Lord: I don't get the connection,' he said.

'Blest are the pure in heart, for they shall see God.'

'Ah . . . you mean we have to hold the telescope to the good eye to see.' Peter beamed at his own deduction.

'When your eyes are sound,' said Jesus, 'your whole body is full of light; but when your eyes are no good, your whole body will be in darkness. Make certain, then, that the light in you is not darkness. If your whole body is full of light, with no part of it in darkness, it will be bright all over, as when a lamp shines on you with its brightness.' A party of school-children walked past giggling and scuffing and chewing gum. 'Look at their eyes,' said Jesus softly.

'On the boat . . .' said Matthew. 'The *Victory*, if you please,' interrupted Jesus.

'On the *Victory* . . . I was chatting up this delightful young woman and Peter said to me "Blest are the pure in heart".'

'Well?' asked Jesus, looking hard at him. 'Were your motives entirely pure?' Matthew smiled uneasily.

'And when Peter was coveting the longboat, and James coveting that camera – were their desires pure?'

'Pure greed,' said Peter and hoped that the soft answer might defuse the tension. There was no reply. He stammered on, 'But, Lord, how can we be pure in heart? Aren't our motives always mixed?'

'Yes,' said Jesus.

'Well, that's a bit rough,' said James, beginning to work up one of his tempers. 'If we can't help our motives being mixed, how shall we ever see God?'

'Once there were two men who went up to the Temple to pray: one was a Pharisee, the other a tax collector. . .

'Everyone who makes himself great will be humbled and everyone who humbles himself will be made great. . .

'Purity of heart can only be attained by those who come to God in utter poverty of spirit. . . Sometimes,' he said, 'you will feel as though your very soul is in pain. Everything is in turmoil, no certainties left, nothing. . . Purification is not always painless, but God is with you, preparing you for the vision of his glory. . . Blest are the pure in heart, for they shall see God. . .'

'Lord,' said Peter, 'how will God purify my heart?'

And Jesus looked at Peter with such tender compassion that he almost wept. . .

The Magnificat

About this time Mary set out and went straight to a
town in the uplands of Judah . . .

(Luke 1.39)

The scholars are divided about both the provenance and
origin of the Magnificat. Whoever wrote it – and I see no real
reason to doubt that it could have been Mary herself – was
both a remarkable poet and a radical theologian. I have
placed these meditations in England, and have imagined that
Mary in her old age lived in a cottage in a village near
Glastonbury. Pure romance, I know, but I think that too is a
valid source for prayer.

My soul doth magnify the Lord

'I wonder if it's all a terrible mistake.' She looked old and frail
and tired, and was sitting on the edge of a packing case in a
room that was being cleared by removal men.

'You shouldn't think like that, Mother,' came the reply from
behind a chest of drawers. It was James talking. He was
taking up a carpet. 'You have become very fed up with life in
Town and you need a break – a real break. Fresh air. Rose-
gardens. Blue remembered hills.' (He was being uncharac-
teristically romantic.)

'It's all the things I'd forgotten I had,' she said: 'Trying to
decide what to leave for the dustman and what to take's so

'difficult.' She sighed, pushed a wisp of white hair from her eyes and looked around her.

'You should be more efficient, Mother.' James was always giving that kind of advice. He was an executive of some sort or other.

'But this time, my dear James,' said Mary, 'I have been.'

'You have?'

'Yes.'

'All my most precious things I've put in the top drawer of that chest.'

'And what sort of things?' He was insatiably curious.

'Oh, just things.'

'It's time we had a cup of tea,' said James, changing the subject. 'I'll make it.'

'No,' she said, 'let me – and then whilst I'm doing that you can rummage around in that drawer and see if anything's missing.'

James blushed. His mother seemed to know him through and through.

'Are you sure, Mother?'

'Most certainly.'

She stepped over books and cushions and around chairs and squeezed into the kitchen to make the tea. When she returned, James was sitting on the window-ledge reading a yellowing scrap of paper.

'What's that, James?' she asked.

'Just a sentence on a paper in your handwriting. It says "My soul doth magnify the Lord . . ." and then there are all kinds of crossings out and pencil marks.'

'Oh,' she said. 'This tea's very hot.'

'Who's changing the subject now? I don't see why that paper's so important to keep,' said James. 'One scrap of paper and only one complete sentence.'

'It's very precious to me.'

'Why?'

'If you really want to know, it's a sentence that came leaping into my head when I was expecting your brother.' She said the words 'your brother' as though they had quotation marks around them. Special. With affection.

'I've never understood you, Mother: all this "soul" business. Why use the word? You can't measure a soul. You can't even see a soul. Is your soul in your head or your heart. . .?' He was, in his embarrassment getting quite carried away.

'Yes,' was all she replied – a very, very quiet 'Yes'.

'That's not an answer,' he said, putting the scrap of paper back in the drawer.

'Your soul,' she said, and then paused. 'Your soul is to your body like music is to a guitar – it's the breath of God inside you; the life of God welling up as springs of living waters.'

'Don't mix your metaphors,' said James, tugging at some more of the carpet.

She ignored him. 'Your soul is the value you give to other people.'

James was only half listening now. 'Say that again, Mother.'

'Your soul is the value you give to other people. When you love someone very, very deeply you want all that is best for that person. If you don't love others you lose your own soul. . .'

' "My soul doth magnify the *Lord*",' said James. 'That's what you wrote, not "others" but "the Lord".'

'Of course I did, James. I felt surrounded by God's love when I had "your brother" ' (there were those quotation marks again). 'I felt as though I wanted to sing for ever. I felt unbelievably happy.'

James continued to tug at the carpet. He was now trying not to listen, as he found his mother's explanation touching.

'I discovered in God the joy behind the joy, the peace beyond all understanding. More "me" than I'd ever been before. In tune with the music of God. . .'

He glanced up and saw his mother looking out of the window, tears streaming down her face.

'Come on, Mother,' he said: 'The move to the country isn't going to be that bad. We'll all come to see you.'

'It's not that,' she said, brushing away the tears with the back of her hand. 'It's not that at all.'

He put his arm around her shoulders. 'What is it, then?'

'Old age,' she said. 'The "I wonders" and "might have beens".'

A burly man walked into the room. 'Excuse me, Madam . . . may we now take that chest and put it on the van?'

'Just a moment,' she said. She went to the top drawer and took out the scrap of paper. Folding it very carefully she put it in the pocket of her apron.

'Now you can take it,' she said. 'Thank you . . . and I'll see it in Somerset. In the cottage.' She was willing herself to be brave and cheerful.

'My soul doth magnify the Lord.'

The removal man didn't know what to make of that remark.

'Very probably, Madam,' was all he could say.

'Oh, not "probably": "most certainly". Most certainly . . .'

James, as perplexed as ever, gave a knowing nod to the man and helped him to carry out the chest of drawers.

'She'll be fine once she's settled down again,' he said – but he knew, he really knew that that was nowhere near the truth.

She was the most "settled" person he'd ever known. ' "My soul" ', he said, ' "doth magnify the Lord".'

'You said something, sir?'

'No, nothing . . .' he replied, with an embarrassed smile.

For he hath regarded the lowliness of his handmaiden

It was one of the early days of summer – late May. The sun was shining across a newly-mown lawn. Beyond the lawn was an orchard and beyond that, in the distance, just visible through the apple-tree branches, a small hill rose out of the Somerset plain. Mary was sitting at a wrought-iron table. On it, held down by a plain glass paperweight, were some sheets of paper. In the sun, at Mary's feet, lay a cat stretching in the warmth. A cocker-spaniel came padding out of the house to sit in the shade and flopped exhausted by the effort.

Mary was working a small tapestry.

'Well,' said James, 'this really is idyllic. After your flat in Town I call this paradise.' He leaned back in the faded deck-chair, basking in the sun. 'I always told you that you would take to life in the country, Mother.'

'Don't forget I grew up in a village,' she replied.

'And what are you doing with yourself all day?'

'This and that.'

'Which means?'

'Friends come round for coffee. I do a bit of gardening. I cook. I sew. I write. . .'

'More poetry?'

'Of a sort.'

'What about?'

She indicated the paper on the table: 'When the mood takes me I write.'

'May I see your poem?'

'Of course – but it's really quite old. A poem written a long time ago which I'm trying to bring to mind. In fact, you remember when I moved?'

'Yes.'

'You found a scrap of paper in a drawer?'

'Yes.'

'I'm trying to finish that poem.'

'Ah.'

It was a non-committal sigh. He reached across to the papers on the table and read the words aloud: ' "My soul doth magnify the Lord, and my spirit hath rejoiced in God my saviour. For he hath regarded the lowliness of his hand-maiden" . . . and why did you stop there?'

'I needed time to think.'

In the bushes a blackbird chink-chinked a warning. The cat had gone hunting. The dog remained immobile – great brown eyes filled with remorse for the tiredness of old age.

'What did you want to think about?'

' "Lowliness", James, "lowliness".'

'I shouldn't have thought that lowliness was all that difficult.' He watched the cat returning from its failed hunting expedition.

'You're wrong, James. Lowliness is so difficult to understand. It's living with the truth of your very self. Really living with it. Having no illusions. Facing your self as you really are, and then having a smile about it all.' And Mary smiled – not the smile of self-mockery nor the smile of victory, but the steady serene smile that comes out of intense suffering and intense joy. James was abashed by it and covered his confusion by clearing his throat: Mary continued.

'Lowliness took a lot of learning,' she said. 'I wasn't a bit wise when I was young,' she continued. 'Hopeless, really – "a flibbertigibbet" my mother called me . . . and I'm not wise now, but I do know a little bit about myself . . . and I do know that when the Almighty looks on us he looks at the centre of our being and is gracious to us. Do you know that, James?'

James distracted himself by scratching the dog's ears, and the newspaper slid to the floor. 'Probably, Mother.' He wanted to change the conversation. A bit intense. Not practical enough.

'The thing is, James, God really is gracious . . . it's a lovely word. He loves, forgives, knows, understands, all at one moment . . . and when you have felt the eyes of God searching your soul you no longer have anything to fear. So when I talk about "lowliness" I'm not talking about introspection. Knowing yourself is to discover that you are known by the Almighty. You become aware that for God knowledge and love are one and the same . . . one and the same.'

'And judgement?' asked James. 'If God sees my very soul, will he not judge me?'

There was a long silence whilst Mary looked out at the apple-trees in the orchard.

'But what if his judgement is not to condemn, but to bring life: not to imprison, but free: not to execute, but to release . . . isn't that the searing judgement of God? Not many of us can cope with that – it makes life possible – and who wants that?'

'I think I'll feed the goldfish before I go, Mother,' said James, leaping to his feet and walking over to the pond – where he saw his own reflection, and beneath it, the fish swimming quietly around.

'For he hath regarded,' he said under his breath, 'the lowliness . . .' and to his surprise found himself listening to God. . .

For behold from henceforth all generations shall call me blessed

The parrot in the glass case at the top of the dark stairs was a great favourite. She had brought it all the way from Nazareth and had given special instructions to the delivery men: 'Be very careful with that,' she said.

'Of course, Ma'am: what's his name?'

'Fowl-of-the-Air or "Fofa", for short.'

The men, in their aprons and flat caps, were bemused. . .

'A family story,' she said. It was the parrot she talked to as she dusted the bannisters.

'Lovely morning, Fofa . . . and here I am moving the dust around. I should be outside gardening', or, perhaps when she was calling one of her grown-up children down for breakfast: 'Fofa: you'd think they'd shift their lazy selves once in a while, wouldn't you?'

It was on one such morning that she heard James reply. He was staying for the weekend.

'Mother: we're off to London. . .' he said as he came out of his bedroom. 'I've decided. It's time you saw the sights again. . .'

'Oh, I don't know, James,' she said. 'Will they recognise me? They've got used to me now round here. They don't stare like they used to. In London perhaps I shall have to go through all that publicity again. I hate it. I really do. Being here in this cottage, feeding the hens, taking the dog for a walk, having you and the disciples come to stay. That's lovely. But London – that's another matter. . .'

'I seem to remember,' said James: 'that in that poem you once wrote you said "For behold from henceforth all generations shall call me blessed. . .". So – you can expect the crowds to want to know you. . .'

'James', she said, going back downstairs and towards the kitchen: 'There's all the difference in the world between "blessed-ness" and being treated as a celebrity. To be blessed, you may remember, is to receive grace from God. Unexpected. Unannounced. Undeserved. It is to receive joy at the centre of your soul like a spring of living water. Blessedness is given not made . . . now, come on, have your breakfast. . .'

James drank his coffee and ate his cornflakes and toast. Mary read the morning papers.

'I think, Mother', said James, wiping some marmalade from his fingers, 'that to be called "blessed" by hundreds and thousands of people is a great honour. . .'

'. . . and a kind of burden', she said. 'They don't really know me but they imagine all kinds of good things about me. That's quite a weight, you know . . . if they knew me really, would they say "blessed"?'

'Yes', said James, pouring another cup of coffee. 'Yes . . . undoubtedly, yes.'

'You old flatterer.'

'Not flattery: a statement of the truth. . .'

'Do you know', she said, turning the conversation, 'When Simeon in the Temple said "and a sword shall pierce through your own heart also" I wonder if he said more than he knew. Most people think that that was the sword of the crucifixion . . . well, it was. It was. But it was also the sword of the Resurrection – a sword of such brilliance and glory that it

74

must have been made by angels – and then also it is the sword of recognition. I sometimes so long to be alone, to be ordinary, to be just one of the crowd of women who shop and cook and work – yet, wherever I go I'm always carrying that sword with me. . . Sometimes the Cross and the Resurrection seem to be one and the same. . . Do you know, James, hearts can break with love as well as sorrow? . . . more toast?'

James was looking out of the window. In the background a copper-beech was shimmering in the summer breeze.

'Mother', he said, 'I think you're blessed because you can bear the truth. "Bear" it in the sense of "carry", and "bare" it in the sense of "reveal". That's what blessedness is, isn't it?'

'Probably', she said, beginning to clear the table and rattle the cups. 'Very probably . . . but that's not the main aim of my life – all I want to do is the will of God; obedience-in-love before anything else, and the rest will follow. . .'

She began to run the water into the washing-up bowl.

'. . . but what that rest is he alone knows . . . and sometimes I find that the most comforting mystery of all and sometimes, when my faith wobbles, I simply wonder. . . But then,' she looked towards James (he was in some ways so like his brother), 'I remember how it all began. The message. The vision. The glory . . . and although I can't see the end I believe it will be all right. All right.'

She sat on the kitchen chair. 'My word,' she said, running her hand across her forehead, 'some days I feel so tired, so tired. . .'

75

James took the washing-up cloth from her and stood looking down at her. White haired and tired. Dead tired. But even so, as he said to himself: 'Very, very blessed.'

'We'll forget London,' he said. 'Have a quiet day at home instead. Come on. . .'

'Now that's what I call a real blessing,' she said – and found herself wondering what she might plant in the garden after breakfast. . .

And Holy is his name . . .

The cat, a small tabby with beautiful markings, had been stalking the dog for long enough. First it hid amongst the lavender and came leaping out at great speed just in front of the dog's nose; then it disguised itself amongst the irises and pretended it was in an exotic jungle; but the final insult came when it climbed the young copper-beech and leapt to the ground just behind the benign old spaniel, startling it to canine fury. The latter barked and ran (or at least gave an ancient impression of running), and looked so thoroughly displeased that the cat took refuge on the roof of the stone-built summer-house.

'Tyger', said Mary, 'you are a hopeless and incorrigible cat.' The cat, from its lofty vantage point, looked proudly over all its kingdom and appeared not to hear what Mary had said.

The dog, a liver cocker spaniel of uncertain vintage, was disconsolate: ashamed at being out-manoeuvred by the cat. (The spaniel was known as "Daniel"). Mary continued to walk in the warm sunshine on the arm of her son, James.

They were making their way slowly towards a wrought-iron garden table and two wooden chairs.

'Mother', said James, 'why on earth did you call Daniel, Daniel?'

'Silly, isn't it?' she replied. 'A childish love of rhyme – and because it reminded me of a gorgeous story by Dylan Thomas. Anyway, Daniel the spaniel's a bit gauche, like his namesake. He came from a very good litter – royal connections, I'm told – so I thought Daniel was a good name.'

'And Tyger. Why Tyger for the cat?'

'Ah,' said Mary, 'Daniel is associated with lions: so I wanted a cat to represent the tigers. The only thing I insist on, and it's perfectly ridiculous of me, is that he should be called Tyger with a "y". After Blake', she said, ' "Tyger, Tyger burning bright . . ." What a line. I wish I'd thought of it myself. . . So: I have a dog called Daniel and a cat called Tyger'.

'. . . and a crossword-puzzle mind', said James. They had reached the chairs and now sat in them, looking out across the lawn.

'I just like names,' continued Mary. 'It's a real art finding exactly the right name for something or someone. I know it's not done to think like this – but sometimes I quite envy Eve,' she said. 'Naming all the animals. Imagine: "Hippopotamus", "Rhinoceros", "Baboon". Glorious . . . getting the name exactly right so that it fits. A divine skill. . .'

In the pond in front of them a few ripples broke the surface as a bright red fish came up to snap at a fly.

'I sometimes wonder,' said Mary, 'who called God "God"? There must have been one person a long, long time ago who came up with the name – and it's stuck. . .'

'I suppose,' said James, 'that it was God himself.'

'But he had many names,' said Mary, 'Yahweh . . . Elohim . . . I love the story of Moses asking him his name and that thunderous reply: "I am who I am". The best name ever. . .'

'Except "Emmanuel" ', said James.

'And I sometimes wish,' said Mary, continuing her reverie, 'that I didn't know God's name at all – that it was wrapped in majesty and mystery: a profound and cosmic secret. To know God's name and to use it so lightly is to forget his holiness. . . Perhaps we would do better simply to keep silence and allow our hearts to adore: to wait quietly upon his truth . . . all this babbling familiarity with God can be very unseemly. If God is utterly holy, utterly beautiful, utterly glorious, our words towards him should be measured and honest and good, shouldn't they? We should approach him in love – for love is his name, love is his meaning, love is his being – and in that love is holiness itself. Holiness is love and love is holiness – it's as simple as that, isn't it?'

There was a long pause as James tried to frame a reply, but then Tyger intervened – as cats can intervene – sinuously and quietly stealing the limelight. He stalked an imaginary bird, gave up, ran towards Mary, rubbed against her legs, and then lay in the sunshine on the table.

'I think that cats (and dogs) have a sort of holiness,' she said. 'They are supremely themselves – true through and through to what they are; in the way that God is true to himself, through and through. . . Perhaps that's what holiness really is,' she said. 'Truth and honesty and love in one pure moment – the spark that ignites the Universe . . . "and Holy is his name".'

And his mercy is on them that fear him . . .

A door led from the living room into a stone-flagged passageway – and beyond that down two steps was the shop. The passageway, being cool, was the place where the cheese and bacon were kept, all carefully protected against flies by muslin cloths. It was a favourite part of Mary's house, and the combination of smells and the overheard conversation in the shop ('Terrible weather for the time of year . . .') always had a faint excitement for her.

The shop was run by her unmarried daughter, Ruth – a sprightly woman, a shrewd observer of the village scene, and kindness itself. When children came to the shop Ruth pretended to scold them but then dipped her hand into the sweet jar and said, 'I suppose you'd better have these.' Meanwhile Mary pottered around, rearranging the tins on the shelves, a duster in one hand. There were long periods when no one was in and then she and Ruth could chat.

'They're not afraid any more, are they?'

Mary often began conversations like that. Ruth was assumed to know who 'they' might refer to. She didn't. 'Who's "they", Mother?'

'Children, dear. There was a time when they wouldn't say "boo" to a goose but now they chat away, all smiles and confidence. It's lovely. When I was young I was always afraid of grown-ups – they seemed so big and unpredictable, but not now. Children talk to adults almost like equals and they don't seem afraid at all. . .'

'No', said Ruth, who was trying to add up a column of figures whilst her mother talked. (Mary was now dusting the soap packets; next would be the shoe polish – and then she'd move on to the wooden items, spoons and pegs and hardware.)

'Strange thing, being afraid. Do you suppose that, because children are no longer afraid of grown-ups, they've also lost their fear of God?'

'I don't know, Mother.' Ruth lost her place in the figures and had to begin again.

Mary continued: 'There should be a proper respect – an honest awareness of the distance between themselves and him. Do you know what I mean?'

'Not really,' said Ruth.

'Well, it's not just quantity,' said Mary, flicking the duster over the cat-food tins, 'but quality. Distance can be quality as well as quantity.'

'How?' asked Ruth, but not really listening.

'Compare Rembrandt with your local village oil-painter. The distance is vast – miles apart. The distance between God and us is like that. Qualitatively speaking, we are light-years away from each other.'

Mary was now nearing the fruit with her duster. She picked up an apple, smelt it, said 'Eve wouldn't have bothered with that one' and continued. . .

'When you're in the presence of a Rembrandt there is a touch of fear about it. I mean, the audacious beauty and glory, it takes your breath away. . . And it's like that, only much more so, with God: people will not allow the holiness of God to devastate their hearts. They try to tame him; keep him man-sized. If they really allowed his love room in their lives they might also sense a proper fear . . . and then, oh, then. . .'

She stood gazing out of the window. A man on a bike wobbled past and waved. She waved back. . .

' "Then, oh, then", what?' asked Ruth.

'Then they'd know his mercy,' she said, and began to polish the glass-topped display cabinet furiously.

'And his mercy,' she continued, as she polished, 'is on them that fear him. . .'

Ruth tried to return to her figures, put pencil to paper, looked up, looked at her mother. . . 'You've lost me,' she said, 'You really have. Mercy should not be linked with fear but with love.'

'Then you don't understand the nature of love,' said Mary, 'nor of God. How can I put it? If you try to draw close to the heart of God, you begin by taking a few faltering steps – and it's all very lovely, very, very happy. Then, as you draw closer, you realise that his love has become more holy: sharp, even. Draw closer still and the love becomes fierce and so radiant that you can barely go on, for you see yourself as you really, really are. And at that point in your soul's nakedness you are touched by love and fear at one and the same time, and the truth wounds you. . .'

81

Mary paused for a long while, duster in hand.

'And then,' she said, 'you discover the mercy of God.' (She said the word "mercy" with tender and deep affection.) 'For it's when you are wounded by the knowledge of God, you realise that the wounds are not gashes at all, but wounds of love, wounds of healing. The mercy of God is like the touch of dew on a lawn, or a shaft of sunlight, or a young horse galloping in a meadow: of such beauty and freedom that you want to dance an Alleluia! "And His mercy is on them that fear him",' she said. '– and in that mercy is truth; and in that mercy is wounding; and in that mercy is life eternal. . .'

At which point the shop door opened and in walked a young child clutching some money and looking eagerly at the sweet jar. . . 'Throughout all generations,' she said. 'Have a sweet. . .'

'Thank you, Mary,' said the child, as bold as brass – and Ruth, seeing the expression on her mother's face, simply smiled like an angel.

He hath shewed strength with his arm: he hath scattered the proud in the imagination of their hearts

She was having her mid-morning coffee in the garden. The sun was sufficiently warm to sit in, the wind had dropped, summer was teetering in – on tiptoe, by stealth. Tyger the cat, like all cats, had an instinct for knowing where she was. When she'd gone into the garden he was nowhere to be seen; as soon as she sat down he came padding across the lawn, tail up, miaowing. Mary arranged the chairs so that she sat on one; the cat leaped on to the other.

'Hello, Tyger.'

The cat gazed at her with a mixture of insight and simple-mindedness which was very appealing.

Ruth, the shop being closed for the day, came to join her. She was carrying her cup of coffee. Tyger didn't move as she came closer – laying claim to the territory of the chair.

'Move, Tyger,' said Ruth. The cat looked at her, ignored her, licked its side. 'Come on, Tyger, move and let me sit down.' The cat still didn't budge. With her free hand she moved the chair and tipped him off.

'Cats are so strong-willed, aren't they? If you hadn't tipped him off he wouldn't have moved. Cats,' Mary continued, sipping her coffee, 'are very God-like. It's no wonder the Egyptians had such a thing about them. . . "Oh I am a cat that likes to gallop about doing good".'

(It was a quotation from Stevie Smith.)

Ruth was not really listening; she gazed into the middle distance, attuned to the sound of a blackbird in the rose-garden.

Mary continued: 'Cats are like God because they have his sort of strength.' It was an enigmatic comment and one which she knew Ruth could not ignore – all she had to do was wait.

'In what way can the strength of a cat possibly be compared with the strength of God?' Ruth asked eventually. Tyger had forgiven her for the territorial insult and was rubbing around her ankles. She bent down to stroke him – and he moved just out of reach, lying on his side, scrabbling at the grass, waiting to be tickled. Ruth sighed, put down her coffee, stood up, walked towards Tyger and, bending down, stroked him.

'You've answered your own question,' said Mary, 'haven't you? Tyger, by affectionate cunning, has outwitted you. You are physically much stronger – a great Amazon, but all he had to do was to move just out of reach and you went to him. Isn't that the strength of God? Not force of arms. Not overwhelming majesty – but playful and affectionate persuasion. You didn't have to go to Tyger. You don't have to go to God. He gives you the freedom to reject, and he gives you the divine capacity to respond – but to respond in such a way that you never lose your freedom. Tyger and God are very much alike. . .'

Ruth continued to stroke Tyger, who showed signs of wanting to go exploring. He stood up, arched his back, yawned, walked a few paces away and sat down.

'And is that like God?'

'Undoubtedly,' said Mary: 'Independence – at least the appearance of it, but keeping you within distance. "He hath shewed strength with his arm",' she said, ' "He hath scattered the proud in the imagination of their hearts". . .'

It was another enigmatic statement. Clearly Mary was in a teasing mood herself. Ruth responded.

'I can see God's strength,' she said – 'but what's all this about "scattering the proud in the imagination of their hearts"? Is that like Tyger too – hunting and teasing magpies? If it is, I want none of it.'

84

'If I say "Yes and No" you mustn't be too cross,' said Mary.
' "Yes" because the justice of God is as straight and direct as
Tyger's attack – if I say "No", it's because the attack is not
designed to kill but to convert. The proud need to be scattered so that they don't lose sight of what's important. The
proud obstinately trust the wrong things – either their own
abilities (they think that they are self-created) or their own
possessions (they think that they've deserved them). It's
because God loves them that he scatters them. . .'

'What for?' asked Ruth.

'In the hope that in their lostness they will find him. In the
hope that in their silence they will hear him. In the hope that
in their solitude they will see him coming towards them.
From one angle it looks like justice,' she said, 'and from the
other like love.

   ' "Signs are taken for wonders, 'We would see a sign!'
   The word within a word, unable to speak a word,
   Swaddled with darkness. In the juvescence of the year
   Came Christ the tiger." '

Acknowledgement

The quotation on page 85 comes from 'Gerontion' by T. S. Eliot, and is reprinted from the *Collected Poems of T. S. Eliot* by kind permission of Faber and Faber.